**QTS**

# English for Primary Teachers

## An Audit and Self-Study Guide

**David Wray** and **Jane Medwell**

**EDUCATIONAL**

414 Chiswick High Road
London
W4 5TF

Tel:    020-8996 3333
Fax:    020-8742 8390
e-mail: mail@lettsed.co.uk

## Acknowledgements

Much of the content has been stimulated by, and draws on, national initiatives undertaken in part by the authors on behalf of the TTA and other agencies concerned with standards, oracy, literacy and numeracy. Thanks are due to the staff at University of Exeter School of Education, Homerton College Cambridge, Westhill College Birmingham and the University of Wolverhampton, particularly Christine Doddington, Gill Hackett, Charmaine Hebbard, Anne Thwaites, Keith Warburton, Nigel Woodhead and Roger Woods. Special thanks to Roger Trend in the School of Education, Exeter, for co-ordinating the new QTS series, to Barry Sutcliffe at Topics for project management above and beyond the call of duty, and to Chris Kington of Chris Kington Publishing without whose help and dedication the project would never have been completed.

The first activity in this book relates to Stainthorp, R. (1997) "A Children's Author Recognition Test: a useful tool in reading research." *Journal of Research in Reading*, **20**, pp 148-158.

A CIP catalogue record is available from the British Library

ISBN 1-85805-317-X
Copyright David Wray and Jane Medwell © 1997

Reprinted 1998 (twice), 2000 (twice)

Designed and edited by Topics – The Creative Partnership, Exeter

Printed and bound in Great Britain by The Thanet Press

# Contents

## About the series

The Letts QTS Series offers support for all those preparing to become teachers and working towards Qualified Teacher Status (QTS). The content, teaching approaches and practical ideas are useful for trainee teachers, teacher tutors and mentors, and teacher educators in higher education. Our aim is to be clear, realistic and honest about what learning to teach is all about. The Letts QTS series addresses all of the Standards for QTS and appropriate subject content needed to attain those standards.

Just like the "Standards for the Award of Qualified Teacher Status", this QTS Series has had its own history of change. Also, like the earlier editions of the government's QTS Standards, the earlier editions of the Letts QTS Series are not likely to be of much interest to you as you embark on your professional training! However, please be aware that the documentation you will see as you follow your course of professional training is like that because of previous decisions made about earlier editions. Everything has a past and a future. You might also like to consider what future editions of the government's QTS Standards and the Letts QTS series might look like…

The short series handbook *QTS: A Practical Introduction* gives trainees an overview of the QTS requirements and a more detailed interpretation of each standard.

The main books in the Letts QTS Series offer trainees the chance to audit their knowledge of the content of the subjects, pinpoint areas of further work, and then use support materials to develop their knowledge further. The subjects covered by the Series are English, Mathematics, Science and Information & Communications Technology.

There are two letts QTS series books for each subject:

**Book 1** addresses trainees' subject knowledge at their own level by offering a systematic and comprehensive guide to appropriate requirements of QTS. This allows trainees to check their own knowledge of each of the subjects. Section one provides a comprehensive audit of this subject knowledge and understanding, with helpful feedback and follow-up set out in section two. Having identified any weak areas of subject knowledge, trainees can then use the support materials in section three to develop key ideas and map out their personal learning plan.

**Book 2** for each subject is a handbook of lesson plans, knowledge and methods. This provides details of carefully selected lessons which illustrate effective teaching. It shows how lesson planning and classroom teaching draw on a high level of subject knowledge. It demonstrates how carefully integrated whole-class teaching and group and individual work can be designed to ensure that pupils make progress in their learning.

The Letts QTS Series aims to break down the requirements of QTS into manageable units, so that trainees can evaluate and improve their knowledge of each subject. The books in the series are written in a straightforward way by authors who are experienced teachers, teacher educators, researchers writers and specialists in their subject areas.

**Roger Trend**
**Series Coordinator**

## About this book

The Standards for the award of QTS require newly qualified teachers to be confident and authoritative in the subjects they teach. This demands a level of knowledge including, in the case of English,

- **The nature and role of standard English**
- **The spoken and written language systems of English**
- **How to evaluate texts and language critically**
- **A range of technical terms**

The language systems of English can be further defined at three levels:

**Lexical** (word and sub-word level), including phonology, graphology, how these two systems represent each other, morphology and vocabulary characteristics.
**Grammatical** (sentence level), that is, the grammar of spoken and written English and the functions and conventions of punctuation.
**Textual** (text level), including cohesion, layout and text organization.

This knowledge is extensive and, inevitably, fairly technical. The purpose of this book is to help readers assess for themselves the extent of their own knowledge in this area and to give some direction to readers' attempts to improve their knowledge. It gives no advice about the teaching of this knowledge. This will be found in a subsequent volume in the Letts QTS series.

The book begins with a range of materials through the use of which readers can audit their own knowledge. These materials are grouped to reflect the organization of knowledge described above. The groups are:

**Using and examining texts.** Here the focus is on a critical awareness of a range of texts, including literature, poetry and factual texts.
**Textual structure and conventions.** This group highlights the ways texts are structured to meet particular purposes.
**Grammar and punctuation.** Here the rules and conventions of grammar and punctuation are covered.

**How words work.** The focus here is on word and sub-word features such as morphemes and phonemes.
**Looking at children's language.** This group asks readers to examine closely examples of children's reading and writing in order to tease out their strengths and weaknesses as language users.

Subsequent sections of the book provide an explanation of the answers to the audit materials in section 1 and then go on to suggest some ways in which readers might develop their knowledge in crucial areas.

The book thus provides the reader with a systematic and fairly comprehensive way of meeting the demands of the knowledge component of the new Standards for primary English.

# Auditing your knowledge in English

## Using and examining texts

Assessing your knowledge of children's literature

### Recognizing children's authors

The following list of names contains some who are genuine authors of books for children and some who are not. Try to identify as many of the genuine children's authors as you can.

| | | |
|---|---|---|
| Allan Ahlberg | Gillian Cross | Nina Bawden |
| Arthur Ransome | Helen Andrews | Norma Cooke |
| Bernard Ashley | Helen Cresswell | P.E. Davies |
| Betsy Byars | Ian Lawson | Pamela Wooley |
| Beverley Cleary | J.R.R. Tolkein | Pamela Yeadon |
| C.I. James | Jan Mark | Paul Kaiserman |
| C.S. Lewis | John Shelmadine | Penelope Lively |
| David Henry Wilson | Judy Blume | Peter Massey |
| David Taylor | Kathleen Butterman | Philippa Pearce |
| David Wise | Lewis Carroll | Raymond Briggs |
| Dawn Glennie | Louise Rosenberg | Roald Dahl |
| Diana Rule | Malcolm Adamson | Rosemary Sutcliff |
| Dick King-Smith | Mary Barker | Stephanie Weinberg |
| Duncan Smith | Merle Broxton | Sue Townsend |
| Enid Blyton | Michael Kelly | Susan Edis |
| Florence Parry Heide | Myra Kersner | Terry Pratchett |
| F.R. Smith | Nicholas Fiske | |

For each genuine author you identify, give one example of a children's book he/she has written.

> A key requirement for you as a teacher of primary English is that you should be able to analyse different types of fiction, poetry and non-fiction texts, evaluating their quality and making judgements about them. A first step towards this is developing your knowledge of children's literature.

> Some authors write both for children and for adults. Several of these authors may be known for their children's books *and* for their adult books.

Selecting a range of fiction

### Understanding the range of children's fiction 1

Suggest children's fiction in each of the following categories:

(a) historical fiction
(b) picture books
(c) myths or legends
(d) realistic, modern fiction

> This list represents only a small part of the range of types of children's fiction. What other types of children's fiction can you think of?

Classifying fiction

### Understanding the range of children's fiction 2

Suggest titles which fall into each of the following categories:

(a) texts which challenge traditional gender stereotypes
(b) texts which represent a range of cultural backgrounds
(c) texts written at or before the beginning of the present century
(d) texts in which a range of moral issues are raised for discussion

> Texts listed here will inevitably be ones which challenge children in a number of ways. Such challenging is important if they are to be really extended in their reading.

The textual features of poetry

## Looking closely at poetry

The poem below was written by a Year 5 pupil after hearing several poems about the night and ghostly happenings.

### Night Fears

*Night falls and*
*Darkness drops its deadly veil.*
*Lights twinkle but*
*Still my face turns ghostly pale.*

*Night comes and steals the best*
*And hope is like a parting guest.*

*Eerily and wearily*
*I climb into my bed.*
*Scarily and warily*
*I enter into dread.*

*Night comes and steals the best*
*And hope is like a parting guest.*

*I hate the night and*
*All it brings.*
*Its veil shrouds mystery*
*and evil things.*

*Night comes and steals the best*
*And hope is like a parting guest.*

Find in this poem at least one example of each of the following poetic devices:

| | | |
|---|---|---|
| (a) rhyme | (d) metaphor | (g) personification |
| (b) alliteration | (e) simile | (h) rhyming couplet |
| (c) assonance | (f) chorus | (i) extended metaphor |

> This question is not specifically about the quality of this poem as literature, but simply about literary devices. The question of whether the use of such devices enhances quality is an open one.

Children's poets

## Poets and poetry

Below are listed the names of some well-known poets who write or have written specifically for children.

| | | |
|---|---|---|
| John Agard | Eve Merriam | Michael Rosen |
| Allan Ahlberg | Mary O'Neill | Shel Silverstein |
| Ted Hughes | Gareth Owen | Kit Wright |
| Roger McGough | Brian Patten | |

For each of these poets, give the name of at least one book of poetry they have published.

> For each of these poets, try to think of at least three poems they have written which you might want to share with children.

> There are many more well-known children's poets whose work you should become familiar with.

Poetic forms

## Forms of poetry

Here is a list of five common poetic forms:

- Acrostic
- Couplet
- Haiku
- Limerick
- Sonnet

> Children can sometimes enjoy trying to write to strict forms.

The following five short poems, or extracts from poems, represent an example of each of these forms. Try to match the poems to the forms.

A  *Know, nature's children all divide her care;*
   *The fur that warms a monarch, warmed a bear.*

   (ALEXANDER POPE)

B  *There was an old lady whose folly*
   *Induced her to sit on a holly,*
   *Whereupon, by a thorn,*
   *Her dress being torn,*
   *She quickly became melancholy.*

   (EDWARD LEAR)

C  *When to the sessions of sweet silent thought*
   *I summon up remembrance of things past,*
   *I sigh the lack of many a thing I sought,*
   *And with old woes new wail my dear Time's waste.*
   *Then I can drown an eye, unused to flow,*
   *For precious friends hid in death's dateless night,*
   *And weep afresh love's long since canceled woe,*
   *And moan th'expense of many a vanished sight;*
   *Then I can grieve at grievances foregone,*
   *And heavily from woe to woe tell o'er*
   *The sad account of fore-bemoaned moan,*
   *Which I new pay as if not paid before,*
   *But if the while I think on thee, dear friend,*
   *All losses are restored and sorrows end.*

   (WILLIAM SHAKESPEARE)

D  Lobster
   *Late in the evening my claws are sharp and ready,*
   *On the sea in my shell I wait.*
   *Before my claws will open I will polish them till they shine.*
   *Sagging in the mist, a starfish is asleep*
   *Though I wait till my enemy comes.*
   *Evening stars brighten the green waters, but still I wait.*
   *Retaining my courage, I see the crab slowly scampering over.*

   (CHRISTOPHER, AGE 10)

E  *old pond ...*
   *a frog leaps in*
   *water's sound*

   (MATSUO BASHO)

### Looking at bias in text

The following are two accounts of the battle of Vegkop which took place in Southern Africa in 1836.

The first account is that given in the 1980 South African primary history textbook.

All texts are biased because they are all written by someone who has views about and attitudes towards the subject about which he/she is writing.

*The trekkers hurried into the laager and closed the entrance. All around were the Matabele hordes, sharpening their assegais, killing animals and drinking the raw blood. Sarel Celliers offered up a prayer.*

*When the enemy made a savage attack, the defenders fired volley upon volley into their ranks. All helped. The women and children loaded extra guns and handed them to the men. After a fierce battle, the Matabele fled with their tails between their legs. The voortrekkers gave thanks to God for their deliverance.*

Which side in the battle does the writer of this account want you, the reader, to favour?

Identify some of the ways in which language is used in this account to try to persuade you to favour one side.

Who would you say won this battle? How can you tell?

The second account comes from the 1988 Reader's Digest *Illustrated History of South Africa*.

*The trekkers' first major confrontation was with Mzilikazi, founder and king of the Ndebele. In 1836 the Ndebele were in the path of a trekker expedition heading northwards ...*

*The Ndebele were attacked by a Boer commando but Mzilikazi retaliated and the Boers retreated to their main laager at Vegkop. There, after a short and fierce battle, 40 trekkers, thanks to their guns and an efficient reloading system, succeeded in beating off an attack by 6000 Ndebele warriors. 400 Ndebele were killed and the trekkers' sheep and cattle herds were virtually annihilated.*

List some of the ways in which a different impression of the battle is conveyed in this account.

Try to list the events which you feel fairly sure did happen during the battle of Vegkop in order of their occurrence.

From this account who would you say won this battle?

What evidence from the text makes you think this?

Now you have analysed two texts which seem to be about the same event but which tell different stories, try to list some of the features of language which may affect the reader's response to a purportedly factual text.

> **Contrasting texts on the same topic**

> Even though you may feel that one of these texts is more likely to be true than another, you have no real way of knowing. All texts are biased.

> Bias may be deliberate or unintentional.

### Using texts to teach linguistic features
Examine the following text, which is an extract from a longer story and might be a text you would use with Year 5 or 6 pupils.

*"What on earth?" I shouted, my eyes on stalks as I tried to take in the scene. "It's like a battlefield in here!" And it was. And do you know, my sister looked like she was enjoying it.*

*She was sitting, Buddha-like, on the floor amid the debris of our bedroom, or what used to be our bedroom. The bedclothes strewn across the floor told the story of an afternoon of chaos. She'd had her friends round!*

*Well, if that was what having friends round meant, she could jolly well keep it. Her friends must be like the Mongol hordes. I made a mental resolution never to leave her alone again.*

This text could be used to draw the pupils' attention to a range of linguistic and stylistic features which you might wish to emphasize as part of language study.

List as many of these linguistic and stylistic features as you can. Do not include graphophonic features such as sound-symbol relationships, or simple punctuation features such as full stops and capitalization.

Try to find features at three levels, and for each feature you find, give an example of where it occurs in the text:

**Linguistic features at the text level**

(a) whole text level – e.g. the text is a narrative. It is written in the past tense and from the point of view of a person.

**Linguistic features at the sentence level**

(b) sentence level – e.g. exclamation marks used to indicate emphasis, as in "What on earth!"

**Linguistic features at the word level**

(c) word level – e.g. the use of suffixes to indicate past tense, as in "I shout**ed**".

> Simply because a text includes a particular linguistic or stylistic feature does not in itself make it a suitable vehicle for teaching such features. What else would influence your decision to use a text in this way?

**Text readability**

### Looking at text difficulty
There are a number of features, at several levels, which can affect how difficult a text is to read.

List as many of these features as you can.

> Readability is the term used to describe the level of difficulty of a particular text. It can be influenced by a number of features, some to do with the reader and some textual.

## Textual structure and conventions

**What makes a narrative?**

### Looking at narrative
The following passage is a narrative.

> *The train pulled into the station. It stopped at the platform. Then the carriage doors opened and some passengers alighted. The sixteen people who were waiting to travel now boarded the train. Soon the carriage doors were closed. The train left the station and then continued on its journey.*

(a) What are the language features of this text which make it a narrative?

**What makes a story?**

(b) Would you describe this text as a story?

(c) If not, what are the features of story that it lacks?

> Think of stories you know well. What do they have which this narrative does not?

### Story structure
Take two stories you know well. You might, for example, choose fairy stories such as *Red Riding Hood* or *Sleeping Beauty*.

Looking at the structure of stories

Analyse each story using the entries in the following grid:

|  | STORY 1 | STORY 2 |
|---|---|---|
| The title of the story |  |  |
| What is the setting of the story? |  |  |
| List the main characters in the story. |  |  |
| Sketch out the main events in the story. |  |  |
| What is the main problem faced by the characters in the story? |  |  |
| How is this problem resolved? |  |  |

This is a useful exercise to do with children. You might lead on from it by getting them to compose their own stories using the grid as a planning device.

### Looking at non-fiction texts

Below are six examples of non-fiction texts written by primary school children (original spellings have been retained). These texts represent examples of each of the six main genres of factual text. These genres are as follows:

Non-fiction genres

- Recount
- Report
- Explanation
- Instructions
- Persuasion
- Discussion

You might question whether this list of genres represents the bulk of non-fiction texts. A discussion of this can be found on pp.65–6 in *Developing your knowledge*.

Match each text to the appropriate genre.

For each text, answer the following:
(a) What are the main structural features of this text genre?
(b) What are the main language features of this text genre?

Children can learn quite a bit by analysing texts in this way. Try this activity with some children and see if they can spot the genres.

A  *The issue I would like to discuss is whether smoking is bad for you. Some people think that it is alright to smoke but other people say that it is bad for your health.*

*Some people think that smoking is enjoyable. They like having cigarettes. They say it gives you cool looks and that it helps you to concentrate on things better. Children think it is cool when they see their friends and parents smoke and they see children on films and T.V. programmes smoking.*

*Children smoke so that they look older and so they can get into pubs and clubs.*

*Other people think that it gives you heart disease and lung cancer, and it damages your health. When a lady is pregnant, it could kill her baby.*

*Smoking makes you smell horrible and some people say it can lead to drugs. It is a habit you can't get out of and it's a waste of money. If people fall asleep when they are smoking it could cause a fire.*

*I think that because there are more arguments against it is better not to smoke.*

B  **OUR TRIP TO EXETER MUSEUM**

*On Tuesday the 1st February we went on a school trip to a Roman museum in Exeter.*

*First of all we split in to 2 groups. Then my group went upstairs. We looked at Roman tiles, bits of pottery, jawbones, a deer antler, a coin, sheep bone, and a bit of mosaic. We saw a tile which, before it was baked, a dog walked over and it had paw prints on it. When we went downstairs into the Roman kitchen which had been reconstructed from information from the ground. We did some observational drawings. Then we each had a turn at grinding the flour. The guide who took us around told us to look for a mysterious animal that the Romans ate. I was the first person to find out what it was. It was a hedgehog.*

*Then we went to another museum. It was much better than the first because the man who took us round was funny and we allowed to try on Roman armour. We handled the weapons as well. There was a sword, a dagger and a pilon. The armour was a breast plate, a shield, a helmet and a belt made with leather and chingles. The bits they hadn't got were the helmet, dagger and shield. Then we looked at a part of a mosaic. Then we went home.*

*It was a good trip. I liked the armour.*

C  **OBJECT OF GAME**

*The object of the game is to get to the finish with all of the items.*

**EQUIPMENT**

*For the game you will need 1 dice 2–4 counters the 15 item cards.*

**HOW TO PLAY**

*1. Each player chooses a counter and the person who throws a six first starts.*
*2. After you have thrown the dice move the number spaces it says on it.*
*3. If you land on a shop pick up one item card if not carry on. If you land on a space which says lose something place the item it says in the lost item space.*
*4. If you have not got all the cards by the time you have got to the finish keep going round until you have got them. This game is for two–four players.*

D  **LUNGS**

*Our lungs are organs in our body which do the breathing.*

*The lungs are divided into sections called Lobes. There are 2 lobes in the left lung, and 3 lobes in the right lung. Inside each lobe, the lung tubes split and split again, and soon look like this:*
[here the author had drawn a diagram]

*At the end of the lung is a 'bubble' called an alveolur. When we breathe in, the oxygen enters our blood via the alveolur, and when we breathe out, the carbon dioxide leaves us in the same way. When we smoke, the Alveoli get clogged up with tar, so we cannot breathe properly.*

E  *THE WATER CYCLE*

*The water cycle is about what happens to water. I want to explain where rain comes from.*

*To begin with the sun shines on the sea and turns it into water vapour and the water vapour rises up into the sky. Next the wind blows it and it turns into Clouds. Then as it gets colder the water vapour condenses back into water. This falls as rain. It runs down the hills and under the earth and into the rivers and seas. Finally it starts again.*

F  *I think that building houses on the old school field is a bad thing. I have several reasons for thinking this like the wildlife and the youth club.*

*My first reason is that it would be destroying wildlife on the field because of all the digging and when the people move in the noise, the light and other things.*

*A further reason is the Youth club would not like it because they use the field for games and other things. And they might disturb the people in the houses.*

*Furthermore there are enough houses in the village. We do not need anymore. It would just be a waste of space. (We need that space)*

*Therefore although some people think it would be a good thing to because it would create more homes I think I have shown lots of reasons why it is not a very good idea to build more houses here especially on the old school field.*

**Paragraphs and topic sentences**

## Paragraphs

The following passage about dinosaurs is presented here as one single paragraph. Originally the passage was written as three separate paragraphs.

*Dinosaurs were the biggest animals that ever lived. They walked the earth many millions of years ago but are now extinct. Yet scientists know quite a lot about dinosaurs, including what they looked like and even what they ate. How do scientists know these things? The main sources of information about dinosaurs are the fossilized remains which have been found in many parts of the world. Some of the very first dinosaur fossils to be uncovered were found in Britain in the cliffs at Lyme Regis. They were found by a local collector, Mary Anning. From examining dinosaur fossils scientists have been able to work out a lot about the dinosaurs themselves. Some fossil skeletons, for example, have very big hind legs but tiny fore legs. This suggests that these dinosaurs must have walked on their hind legs only. Some fossil skeletons have very large sharp teeth. In others the teeth are smaller and less sharp. From this scientists can work out what these dinosaurs probably ate and whether they were meat eaters or plant eaters.*

Suggest where you think the paragraph splits would originally have been.

For each split you suggest, give a reason why you think the split should occur at that point.

> You might find this rather difficult. There are no absolute rules about paragraphing. If you disagree with the solution given on p.35, argue a case for your own solution.

Paragraphs usually have topic sentences. Which do you think are the topic sentences in each of the paragraphs you have now split this passage into?

### Textual cohesion

In the following extract, (from Williams, G. 1990, *Magic*, Macmillan) several forms of cohesive ties are used to bind the meanings of the text together.

> *When seekers reached the shrine at which they hoped to be given divine guidance, they would find a 'medium' or person appointed to act for the local god or gods. The medium was protected by a number of priests or priestesses. Those wanting guidance were allowed to approach the medium only at a certain fixed time – on the seventh day of the month, perhaps, or on the day believed to be the birthday of a god. They had to take with them some suitable offerings – rich cakes, possibly, or beasts that could be sacrificed.*

In the first line, for example, some cohesive links are:

- *which* refers to *shine* earlier in the sentence
- *they* refers to *seekers*

**Identifying cohesive ties**

Analyse in this way the remainder of the cohesive ties in this passage.

Which of these ties, if any, do you think might cause confusion for a primary child reading this passage?

> Cohesive ties are the elements of language which bind texts together.

> It is not only children who sometimes get lost among the complex cohesion of texts, especially factual texts.

### Cohesive ties

There are five main types of cohesive tie:

- lexical
- substitution
- conjunction
- reference
- ellipsis

**Looking at cohesion in texts**

In the following texts, the words and phrases in bold type indicate the cohesive ties between or within sentences. For each text, identify the type of cohesive tie highlighted. For example, "Text A includes an example of ellipsis" (it does not!).

A *It is important that **milk** is put into clean bottles. Flies like drinking **milk** and they can carry disease.*

B *The **Queen** is the formal head of state. In practice, **her** rule is carried out by an elected parliament.*

C *When the weather was wet, **it was easy to get stuck in the mud**. Because of **this**, many carriages were very late arriving.*

D *He looked at the **bits of stone** carefully. Some of them were roughly the right shape but **some** would be useless.*

E ***Car tyres** eventually wear out and new **ones** have to be fitted.*

F *I was wondering whether it would **be possible to reach the summit before night**. If **it was**, we would be a lot safer.*

G *The headteacher said **that was the last test we would have to do**. We all fervently hoped **so**.*

> This is quite technical language. You might debate whether you need to know these terms in order to understand the concept of cohesive ties.

H  *"You can do what you wish," replied the knight, "but I will never give in.* **For** *I have made a vow to my lady the Queen."*

I  *The* **fish** *is dipped in batter before being fried: the* **chips** *are simply fried in oil.*

J  *We all assembled on the bank, dripping wet and very cold.* **Then** *the captain began to harangue us.*

### Connectives

Ideas are often linked together in texts by connective words or phrases. There are many forms of connectives. The following list includes a few of these:

- addition
- exemplification
- result
- anaphora
- cataphora
- contradictive
- temporal
- spatial

> It is sometimes assumed that conjunctions such as and, but, etc. are the major form of connective in English. This activity should convince you this is not true.

Each of the sentences below contains an example of one of the above forms of connectives. In each sentence, identify the connective and its type. For example:

*On the other hand, it is true that not all Scots wish their country to become independent.*
'On the other hand' is a contradictive connective.

(a) *This was what he was holding: a large pistol pointed in my direction.*

(b) *He said he liked rowing and that this was because of his schooldays.*

(c) *Peter liked bread and jam but James would only eat plain bread.*

(d) *At the same time the Indians were circling the wagons yelling and whooping.*

(e) *John was similarly unhappy about the way events were unfolding.*

(f) *Behind that wall, Peter knew, a dozen armed men were waiting expectantly.*

(g) *Thanks to John's foresight, nobody was hurt during the difficult crossing.*

(h) *Billy certainly did not like the experience, that is to say, he absolutely hated it.*

## Grammar and punctuation

### Parts of speech

*Identifying parts of speech*

Read the following passage which is the introductory section of a short story.

> *Parts of speech* is the term you will most likely be familiar with. The term *word class* is now more widely used, however.

1  *"In an hour I'll be on the train," she said. They were lying in the long*
2  *grass in the field behind the house. It had been very quiet.*

3  *"In two hours I'll be having my interview." He did not reply. She*
4  *considered that the sun absolved him, however.*

*Types of connectives*

5 *She sat up and began to gather together her scattered sandals and*
6 *clothes and the remains of her lunch. Her head ached from the sun*
7 *and the wine.*

8 *"Shouldn't think I'll get it, do you?" she said and touched him with*
9 *her foot where his shirt hung open.*

10 *"Mmmmm? ... You won't be able to get up on time if you do," he said*
11 *with evident satisfaction, without opening his eyes.*

12 *She tried to concentrate on the impossible truth that her presence was*
13 *required in two hours time on the other side of the town by another*
14 *person, a person she did not know. She tried to persuade herself that*
15 *she wasn't as convinced of failure in this venture as in those others she*
16 *had only contemplated.*

17 *She stood up in the glare from the grass and the pain swung to the*
18 *back of her skull. She did not say, "I'm going in now to get ready."*

19 *When she returned he was still lying there, his arm over his eyes.*

20 *"Are you in this evening?" she said for want of anything better. His*
21 *grunt made her no wiser.*

22 *"I thought I might go and see that film."*

23 *"Who with?" he said, spreading his hot smile of contempt over the*
24 *question as the heat of the day had sat upon her will.*

25 *"Well, there's Tom, there's Dick and there's Harry," she said, "three*
26 *fine men," and struggled into the house in alien interview shoes.*

27 *Sarcasm, fruit of pain.*

Answer the following questions about this passage:

(a) Find the following:

adjectives in line 1, line 5, line 11 and line 12
adverbs in line 5, line 9 and line 19
verbs in line 4, line 9, line 16 and line 19
conjunctions in line 5 and line 17
pronouns in line 1, line 8, line 15 and line 24

(b) List all the pronouns in the first 10 lines.

(c) List all the proper nouns in the passage.

(d) List the prepositions in lines 17–18.

(e) Find six abstract nouns in the passage and six concrete nouns.

(f) Some of the following verbs from the passage are transitive verbs
and some are intransitive verbs. Decide which is which. For example,
*reply* is intransitive.

| | |
|---|---|
| *lying* (line 1) | *opening* (line 11) |
| *ached* (line 6) | *returned* (line 19) |
| *touched* (line 8) | *made* (line 21) |

**Word classes** *(margin label)*

**Transitive and
intransitive verbs** *(margin label)*

| | |
|---|---|
| **Verb tenses** | (g) In which tense is each of the following verbs being used in the passage? |

       *were lying* (line 1)           *I'm going* (line 18)

       *considered* (line 4)          *had sat* (line 24)

       *won't be able* (line 10)

| | |
|---|---|
| **Clauses and phrases** | **Looking at clauses and phrases** |

Answer the following using the passage given earlier:

(a) These extracts from the passage are either phrases or clauses. Decide which is which. For example, *in an hour* is a phrase.

    *They were lying in the long grass* (lines 1–2)
    *that the sun absolved him* (line 4)
    *on the other side of town* (line 13)
    *When she returned* (line 19)
    *in this venture* (line 15)
    *to the back of her skull* (lines 17–18)

(b) Explain what you think is the difference between a clause and a phrase.

(c) Each of the following extracts contains a main clause and a subordinate clause. Identify which is which.

    *She considered that the sun absolved him*
    *touched him with her foot where his shirt hung open*
    *She tried to persuade herself that she wasn't as convinced of failure in this venture*

(d) How many clauses are there in each of the following extracts from the passage?

    *They were lying in the long grass in the field behind the house*
    *She sat up and began to gather together her scattered sandals and clothes and the remains of her lunch*
    *You won't be able to get up on time if you do*
    *spreading his hot smile of contempt over the question as the heat of the day had sat upon her will*

> Be careful not to get confused here between phrases and clauses. There is a very important difference between these.

(e) Find the following phrases in the passage:

    an adjective phrase in line 2
    a noun phrase in line 5
    a verb phrase in line 5
    an adverb phrase in line 6
    an adjective phrase in line 17
    a noun phrase in line 23
    a verb phrase in line 19

| | |
|---|---|
| **Sentence types and their language features** | **Sentence types** |

There are four main types of sentences:

- statements     • questions     • commands     • exclamations

Make up a sentence of each of these types.

For each type, list the language features (apart from punctuation) which allow you to distinguish these one from another.

........................................................................................................................

**Punctuation**

(a) There are two full stops in the following sentence. Explain the grammatical function of each of these.

> *Dr. Gregory rushed round to the house as quickly as she could.*

(b) Explain why it is correct to use full stops in *B.C.* and *a.m.* but why these are not necessary in *NATO* and *WRAF*.

(c) Explain the purpose of the three full stops in the middle of the following sentence.

> *"I think that's true but then again ..." replied the chief in a puzzled voice.*

(d) In the following sentences commas are used for different purposes. Explain the grammatical function of the commas in each sentence.

> *When I go fishing I use worms, bread, flies and maggots for bait.*
>
> *Worms, especially the smaller ones, make wonderful bait.*
>
> *Large, wriggly, fat earthworms do not make good bait.*
>
> *If you cannot find the smaller worms, then maggots are the next best bet.*
>
> *Maggots, which are usually white, wriggle and attract the fish very well.*
>
> *You can buy maggots from The Fishing Shop, 24 High Street, Anglertown.*
>
> *"Why," you may say, "would I need to go to that shop?"*
>
> *I would reply, dear angler, that it is simply the best place.*
>
> *In my time I must have bought over 10,000 maggots there.*

(e) All capital letters have been removed from the following passage. Put the capital letters back appropriately and give an explanation for the decisions you make.

> *the u.s.a. is an excellent destination for holidays. (it is also becoming cheaper to get there from britain.) skiing is a very popular sport in the north and the west but if you go south you will find the weather is too warm for snow. I went skiing in lake tahoe with uncle bill last year. my uncle had a fright when he almost fell into the lake. the canadian instructor had to make a rapid u-turn to help him out of the crevasse he had fallen into. the event was reported in the lake tahoe times and several times after that bill was stopped by interested readers. although uncle bill has a ph.d. he says he felt very foolish. I said to him, "you'll have to take more care in future."*

(f) In the following sentences an **X** is used to indicate the presence of either a colon or a semi-colon. Decide which of these punctuation marks is correct in each sentence and explain the reason for your choice.

---

**Full stops**

**Commas**

**Capital letters**

**Colons and semi-colons**

---

The punctuation will usually signal some of these sentence types. Question and exclamation marks are important written clues but, of course, they don't appear in speech.

It should be noted that punctuation marks such as the full stop have a grammatical role to play in a sentence. They are not just there to tell you when to take a breath!

Commas also have a grammatical function. Telling pupils that a comma simply indicates a short pause is to mislead them.

This activity should convince you that there are few rules in the use of language which are universally true. It does all depend upon context.

*Debbie dropped her bag and out spilled the contents **X** car keys, wallet, calculator and a rather crumpled handkerchief.*

*They talked all day without mentioning the one topic on all their minds **X** the robbery.*

*I once had a Jaguar car **X** it was the best I ever drove.*

*Someone had been through the shelves and cleared away all the old books **X** so the library now contained only new, untorn and up to date volumes.*

**Quotation marks**

(g) The following sentences have had all their double and single quotation marks removed. Rewrite these sentences, replacing the quotation marks appropriately.

*I don't really know, he said, whether this year's drought will lead to higher prices.*

*I am firm, you are stubborn, he is pig-headed.*

*Before you get into this to boldly go stuff, let me warn you I'm a very nervous traveller.*

*The poem chosen for the class to study was The Raven by Edgar Allan Poe.*

*Have you never read The Raven? I asked the children incredulously.*

> How do we manage when we need to use two sets of quotation marks at the same time?

**Apostrophes**

(h) The following sentences have had their apostrophes removed. Rewrite each sentence, placing the apostrophe in the appropriate place. Explain the rule that is being applied in these sentences.

*Dont go too near the water.*

*I wonder if shed mind getting that for me.*

*Its very unlikely that I will have the time in the next day or so.*

*Now youre sure we cant do anything else for you?*

*Shall we go to the fishnchip shop to get our lunch?*

> The apostrophe is perhaps the most widely misused punctuation mark in English.

(i) In the following sentences the apostrophes have also been missed out but they follow a different set of rules. Rewrite the sentences replacing the apostrophes and explain the rules you are using to do this.

*John Lennons assassination shocked the world.*

*Teachers skills lie in being able to spot pupils problems quickly and then do something about them.*

*Childrens clothes are much cheaper than adults.*

*This is clearly somebodys field that we are walking through.*

*The man was selling shoes, books and several of his daughters unworn dresses.*

(j) In the following sentences, apostrophes have been used but there is some controversy over whether these are correct or not. For each sentence, explain why you think the apostrophe is, or is not, correct.

*Try not to use too many and's in your writing.*

*Mind your p's and q's.*

*Cross the t's and dot the i's.*

*Life was much easier in the 1960's.*

**Dialect, accent and standard English**

(a) Give definitions of the three terms:

- dialect
- accent
- standard English

Looking at dialect

(b) The following passage has been transcribed in such a way as to give a good clue as to how it was actually spoken in a regional dialect.

> *"Ah's not agin dogs. Ah used tioown yan missen yance. Her neame were Jade, an' she were a reet grand dog. She used ti tak ma fer a walk ivvery day wi'oot fail, rain or shine, whether Ah wanted ti goa oot or not. Ti tell t'truth, tekkin' her oot wor a bit of a drag: she dragged ma throo bushes, hedges, trees, ponds – Ah jist cudn't control her. When Ah were finally allowed ti goa back hoam – usually when she were feeling hungry – t'naybors'd phoned police. They thowt Ah'd bin mugged. They worn't far wrong, nayther."*

The transcription is also trying to represent accent features. Be careful not to confuse these with dialect features.

Pick out the features in this passage which you think indicate dialect characteristics.

Rewrite the passage using standard English grammar and vocabulary (and spelling).

Using standard English

(c) The following is a transcript of part of the Red Riding Hood story told by a London girl whose parents originated from Jamaica.

> *All of a sudden she see a wolf. The wolf say, "Where you going little red riding hood?" She say, "I going to my grandmother house." "And where you grandmother house?" "Up on the other side of the wood." So he say, "OK then, little red riding hood, I go see you." And off he run.*

Describe the ways in which this girl's use of grammar differs from standard English.

Would you consider this girl's use of language to be incorrect or not?

English dialects

(d) Here is a list of some of the common ways in which English dialects differ from standard English grammar. Give an example, from English dialects, of each feature mentioned.

- multiple negation
- past tense verb forms
- relative pronouns
- demonstrative pronouns
- personal pronouns
- forms of the verb 'to be'

# How words work

Syllabification

**Phonology – the sound system of spoken words**

(a) Segment the following words into syllables:

Example: *wig / wam*

|  |  |  |
|---|---|---|
| *bungalow* | *window* | *magnificent* |
| *computer* | *charity* |  |

How did you decide where to split the words into syllables?

(b) When words are pronounced some syllables are stressed and others are unstressed. Identify the stressed syllables in the following words:

|  |  |  |
|---|---|---|
| *supermarket* | *marmalade* | *secrete* |
| *lonely* | *basket* | *refrigerator* |

> English is different from many languages in not having a universal set of rules about stress. This is one reason why English causes difficulties to people learning it as a foreign language.

(c) Placing the stress on certain syllables can affect the meaning of words. Example <u>con</u>*vict* and *con*<u>vict</u>. Identify two more pairs of words where the stress on different syllables indicates different meanings.

Unstressed vowels – the schwa

(d) Identify the schwa sounds in the following words:

|  |  |
|---|---|
| *above* | *scenery* |
| *suppose* | *sofa* |

> The schwa is an unstressed vowel. It is the most common sound in English.

Onset and rime sounds

(e) Split the following words into onset and rime sounds:

|  |  |  |
|---|---|---|
| *string* | *cat* | *building* |
| *zigzag* | *fire* |  |

> Onsets and rimes are sub-parts of syllables. They are important in the process of learning to read.

Looking at rhyme

(f) We say that words rhyme when the final syllables sound the same. However, these syllables may be spelt differently. Example: *moon* and *tune*. Identify three more pairs of words which rhyme but have differently spelt final syllables.

(g) Words may rhyme when more than one of the final syllables sound the same. Example: *battery* and *flattery*. Identify two pairs of words which rhyme because two or more syllables are the same.

The phonemes of English

(h) The alphabet contains 26 letters. How many phonemes (speech sounds) do these represent? How many are vowels and how many are consonants?

(i) Some phonemes are represented by a combination of letters. Identify the letter combinations in the words below which represent phonemes:

|  |  |  |
|---|---|---|
| *dish* | *walking* | *choice* |

(j) How many phonemes are there in the following words?

|  |  |  |
|---|---|---|
| *that* | *swing* | *apple* |
| *fisher* | *mishap* |  |

(k) Segment the following words into phonemes:
Example b/u/n/g/a/l/ow

    *window*        *ready*        *charity*

**Blends, digraphs and trigraphs**

(l) Which of the phonemes highlighted in the words below are consonant blends and which are consonant digraphs or trigraphs?

| *shirt* | *match* | *bring* |
|---|---|---|
| *where* | *chip* | *this* |
| *train* | *split* | *fright* |

**Long and short vowels**

(m) In the words below, which of the highlighted vowels are long and which are short?

| *can* | *bed* | *rut* | *hid* | *rot* |
|---|---|---|---|---|
| *cane* | *cede* | *rude* | *hide* | *rote* |

What rule applies to the pronunciation of the vowels underlined above?

**Digraphs and diphthongs**

(n) In the words below some of the highlighted vowel pairs are digraphs and some are diphthongs. Indicate which are which.

| *fail* | *leonine* | *leopard* |
|---|---|---|
| *pain* | *hear* | *height* |
| *ear* | *speech* | *brooch* |
| *bread* | *toy* | |

(o) Which of the words below have an irregular sound-symbol correspondence?

| *bough* | *mention* | *like* |
|---|---|---|
| *branch* | *balm* | *tongue* |

**Graphology – the alphabetic spelling system**
(a) How many graphemes represent the alphabet?

(b) Which are the five most frequently used and the five least frequently used letters in the alphabet?

(c) Each grapheme can be represented by a number of different letter shapes (graphs). Give two reasons why this is so, with examples.

(d) Some combinations of graphemes represent phonemes. Example: long /e/ as in *meet*, *sheep*, etc. Choose four words which include the long /e/ sound but do not represent it using <ee>.

(e) Identify as many spellings as possible for the following phonemes:

| /a/ in play | /ow/ in cow |
|---|---|
| /i/ in line | /er/ in bird |

(f) Some patterns of graphemes appear regularly in written English and represent the phonemes of spoken English. Example: *cat, mat, bat*. Give three letter strings which are phonemically regular.

**Graphemes**

| | |
|---|---|
| **Spelling strings** | (g) Visually regular spelling strings may represent a number of phonemes. Example: ei in *their, weir, weight, Eiger*. Give examples of three other common spelling strings which are not phonemically regular. |

(h) Which graphemes may be silent in words? Give five examples.

**Homographs**

(i) Give two examples of pairs of words which are homographs.

> English is clearly not a language with a regular phoneme-grapheme correspondence. Other languages such as Finnish and Welsh are much more regular.

........................................................................................................

**Morphology – word meanings, structure and derivations**

**Morphemes**

(a) Segment the following words into the smallest units of meaning (morphemes). Example: *un–happi–ness*.

> Morphemes are the smallest unit of grammar.

| | | |
|---|---|---|
| *houses* | *cat* | *edible* |
| *different* | *skipping* | *revised* |

**Stems, prefixes and suffixes**

(b) Identify the stem, prefixes and suffixes in the words below:

> This is a useful technique for children to learn. It can mean that learning one word will enable them to read several others.

| | | |
|---|---|---|
| *unfaithful* | *undifferentiated* | *inappropriateness* |
| *antiperspirant* | *supercharged* | *disappearing* |

(c) What are the meanings of the prefixes in the words below? Can you suggest other prefixes which have similar meanings for other words?

| | | |
|---|---|---|
| *antebellum* | *submarine* | *transatlantic* |
| *antifreeze* | *postnatal* | *decode* |

(d) Identify the ways in which the suffixes change the stems of the words below. Can you define two categories of change?

| | | |
|---|---|---|
| *cats* | *greatest* | *promotional* |
| *babies* | *higher* | *jumped* |
| *barely* | *rationalize* | *teacher's* |

(e) Identify the inflectional suffix in each of the words below and explain its function. Example: *faster* – the -er suffix makes the adjective comparative.

| | |
|---|---|
| *frogs* | *helped* |
| *being* | *highest* |

(f) The following are derivational suffixes which change the word class of a stem. Example: *life* (noun) + *like*(suffix) = *lifelike* (adjective).

| | |
|---|---|
| *-en* | *-ize* |
| *-ly* | *-al* |

Use these suffixes to create a related word in a different word class from each of the following stems. Identify the original and final word classes of each word.

| | |
|---|---|
| *rough* | *fiction* |
| *high* | *rational* |

(g) Add the appropriate past tense suffixes to the verbs below. Identify the convention or rule which applies to the change of tense.

| | | |
|---|---|---|
| *bat* | *rate* | *utter* |
| *hope* | *rebel* | *need* |
| *omit* | *rain* | |
| *hop* | *open* | |

(h) Add the appropriate plural suffixes to the nouns below. Identify the convention or rule which applies to the creation of each of these plurals.

| | | |
|---|---|---|
| *cat* | *inch* | *half* |
| *baby* | *monkey* | *potato* |
| *frog* | *fish* | *calf* |
| *lady* | *turkey* | *hero* |

## Words

**Homonyms**

(a) Give two homonyms. For each one explain two meanings.

**Homophones**

(b) Give two examples of pairs of words which are homophones.

**Synonyms and antonyms**

(c) Give a synonym and an antonym for each of the words below.

    *nice*            *help*            *top*

(d) Give two compound words.

(e) Give two blend words.

**Word origins**

(f) Try to identify the source of the following words. Example: *forum*, from Latin.

| | |
|---|---|
| *criterion* | *coleslaw* |
| *hammock* | *memorandum* |
| *shampoo* | *ski* |
| *hooligan* | |

> English has borrowed words from a vast number of other languages, current and extinct. Children can be fascinated by this and a lot of useful work can be done on word derivations.

List three more words which have come to English from Latin.
List three more words which have come to English from French.

(g) *Daps* is a word used for sports shoes in some parts of Britain. What other words with this meaning can you name?

# Looking at children's language

**Instruction genre**

### Examining children's writing

*Writing instructions*
After having planted cress seeds with their teacher, a class of Year 2 children were asked to write a set of instructions for growing cress seeds. They had discussed instructions and had decided that somebody else had to be able to follow these.

Below are two examples of the instructions that were written. Original spellings have been retained.

> Clearly if we want to help children produce writing which is appropriate to its purpose, we need ourselves to understand the relationship between writing purpose and form.

EMILY'S INSTRUCTIONS

*get a plate, Three tissues, a Jug of water and seeds. fold Tissues in half on top of each other. put on the plate and put on water. sprinckle seeds on. cover with paper. when it is 9 cm long take paper off and when it is ready cut off.*

JAMES' INSTRUCTIONS

*We had some seeds and Mrs Lewis gave us some seeds in our hands then we sprinkled the seed on the planting plate. Then Mrs Lewis gave us a piece of paper to cover the seeds. We are going to leave them to grow. Every day we will check the seeds to see if they have grown.*

Make an assessment of each of these pieces of writing. How successful do you consider each of them to be? What are your reasons for coming to this conclusion?

**Explanation genre**

*Writing explanations*

These two Year 4 children were asked to explain how rain falls so that someone who had not been in their science lesson could understand how rain is formed.

Both their pieces of writing were titled *Why does the rain fall?* Original spellings have been retained.

MELANIE'S EXPLANATION

*We got a ketle and Lisa and Emma filled it up with water. Then we made it bole. Then Mrs Edwards put the ketle near some glas. It went foggey and the drips fell off the glas. They made rain.*

PETER'S EXPLANATION

*The ran strats as woter in the sea. Bits of woter get hot and flot up to the sky. Becose the sun is hot. But when they get cold they make ran drops. So thy fall down agan and make ran.*

Make an assessment of each of these pieces of writing. How successful do you consider each of them to be? What are your reasons for coming to this conclusion?

**Reading strategies and reading comprehension**

## Examining children's reading

Lisa and William, two Year 4 children, were asked to read aloud the story of *The King's New Clothes*. They were then asked to retell the story they had read. Both their reading and their retelling were recorded and transcriptions of parts of these are given below.

| ORIGINAL STORY | LISA'S READING OF THE STORY |
|---|---|
| What a fuss there was as everyone tried to get a look at the King in his brand new clothes. People climbed up lamp-posts and crawled on to the tops of buildings. The King paraded past as grand as could be. Everyone stared but nobody said a word. | What a ... fuzz there was as ... ever ... tired to get a ... look at the ... King in his ball new ... club. People ... kept up lamp ... posts and ... kept on to the tops of ... bill. The King ... pard past as ... grand as could be ... . Everyone started but ... nobody said a word. |

| LISA'S RETELLING OF THE ABOVE STORY EXTRACT |
|---|
| LISA: He was really ... grand, the King was. They were all looking at the King and they went up ... things ... to see. To look at the King. Up the ... lamp-posts. They were all cheering. They liked ... wanted to see his clothes. They were ... new.<br><br>TEACHER: What do you think might happen next?<br><br>LISA: The King might ... I don't know. |

| ORIGINAL STORY | WILLIAM'S READING OF THE STORY |
|---|---|
| What a fuss there was as everyone tried to get a look at the King in his brand new clothes. People climbed up lamp-posts and crawled on to the tops of buildings. The King paraded past as grand as could be. Everyone stared but nobody said a word. | What a ... fuzz ... fuss there was as everybody tried to go to look at the King in his new clothes. People clambered up lamp ... posts and climbed on to the tops of ... houses. The King went past as grand as could be. Everyone stared but never say ... said a word. |

| WILLIAM'S RETELLING OF THE ABOVE STORY EXTRACT |
|---|
| WILLIAM: Everybody was looking at the King and his new clothes. The King was going somewhere ... like in a procession, like the Queen on telly. They ... all the people ... they were all clambering up things to get a better look, like lamp posts. And on the roof. They'll fall off ... *(laughs)*.They were all quiet ... *(laughs)* .... I expect they could see his bottom.<br><br>TEACHER: What do you think might happen next?<br><br>WILLIAM: He's going to find out and he'll have to grab something to cover up and they'll all laugh and he'll run away. |

**Diagnosing reading**

Use the information you have about Lisa and William to make an assessment of them both as readers. What are their strengths and weaknesses as readers?

Perhaps the most useful assessment technique for reading is the diagnostic procedure known as miscue analysis. This activity contains a version of it.

# Checking your knowledge

How well do you know children's literature?

### Recognizing children's authors

The genuine authors of books for children are listed below. Against each name is given the title of one book he/she has written for children.

All these authors are prolific and have written many books for children.

| | |
|---|---|
| Allan Ahlberg | *Woof!* |
| Arthur Ransome | *Swallows and Amazons* |
| Bernard Ashley | *The Trouble with Donovan Croft* |
| Betsy Byars | *The Eighteenth Emergency* |
| Beverley Cleary | *Ramona the Pest* |
| C.S. Lewis | *The Lion, the Witch and the Wardrobe* |
| Dick King-Smith | *The Sheep Pig* |
| Enid Blyton | *Five go to Kirrin Island* |
| Florence Parry Heide | *The Shrinking of Treehorn* |
| Gillian Cross | *The Great Elephant Chase* |
| Helen Cresswell | *A Gift from Winklesea* |
| J.R.R. Tolkein | *The Hobbit* |
| Jan Mark | *Thunder and Lightnings* |
| Judy Blume | *Forever* |
| Lewis Carroll | *Alice in Wonderland* |
| Nicholas Fiske | *Grinny* |
| Nina Bawden | *The Peppermint Pig* |
| Penelope Lively | *A Stitch in Time* |
| Philippa Pearce | *A Dog so Small* |
| Raymond Briggs | *Fungus the Bogeyman* |
| Roald Dahl | *The BFG* |
| Rosemary Sutcliff | *The Eagle of the Ninth* |
| Sue Townsend | *The Secret Diary of Adrian Mole* |
| Terry Pratchett | *Diggers* |

Selecting a range of fiction

### Understanding the range of children's fiction 1

Here are some titles you might have suggested:

These are titles I found on my shelf. There are, of course, many other possible titles you could have suggested.

(a) historical fiction

| | |
|---|---|
| Joyce Barkhouse | *Pit Pony* |
| Robert Nye | *Beowulf* |

(b) picture books

| | |
|---|---|
| Michael Foreman | *When Dinosaurs Ruled the Earth* |
| Jon Scieska | *The True Story of the Three Little Pigs* |

Selecting an author
and his/her books
to study

(c) myths or legends
    Mollie Hunter     *The Haunted Mountain*
    Phyllis Arkle      *Magic in the Air*

(d) realistic, modern fiction
    Patrick Kinmonth    *Mr. Potter's Pigeon*
    Gene Kemp       *The Turbulent Term of Tyke Tyler*

### Understanding the range of children's fiction 2
Here are some titles you might have suggested:

(a) texts which challenge traditional gender stereotypes
    Gene Kemp       *The Turbulent Term of Tyke Tyler*
    Astrid Lindgren    *Pippi Longstocking*

(b) texts which represent a range of cultural backgrounds
    Peter Dickinson    *The Devil's Children*
    Ann Holm        *I am David*

(c) texts written at or before the beginning of the present century
    Oscar Wilde      *The Selfish Giant*
    E. Nesbit       *Five Children and It*

(d) texts in which a range of moral issues are raised for discussion
    Alan Garner      *Red Shift*
    Nina Bawden     *Carrie's War*

> These books are all very challenging. But do not assume from that that they will be too hard for your children. Given the right kind of support, most junior children will be able to approach these texts.

The textual features of
poetry

### Looking closely at poetry
The following are examples of each of the poetic devices mentioned.

(a) rhyme          *veil/pale*
                    *best/guest*
                    *bed/dread*
                    *brings/things*

Rhyme is a feature of the sounds of word endings. Rhyming words are not necessarily spelt alike.

(b) alliteration      *<u>D</u>arkness <u>d</u>rops its <u>d</u>eadly veil*

Alliteration is the repetition of initial sounds in words, usually consonants.

(c) assonance        *eerily/wearily*
                    *scarily/warily*

Assonance is the repetition of vowel sounds in words. These words do not necessarily rhyme.

(d) metaphor        *Darkness drops its deadly veil*

A metaphor is a figure of speech in which the qualities of one thing are carried over into another, hence the image of a veil dropping is used to describe the onset of darkness.

(e) simile           *like a parting guest*

> Think of ways in which you can explicitly discuss these features with your pupils.

A simile is a special form of metaphor in which the comparison of the two things is made using 'like'.

(f) chorus

*Night comes and steals the best
And hope is like a parting guest.*

A chorus is a repeated sequence of words or lines. The text in between the chorus is referred to as the 'verse'.

(g) personification

*hope is like a parting guest*

In personification an inanimate object or an emotion is described as if it had some of the qualities of a human being.

(h) rhyming couplet

*Night comes and steals the best
And hope is like a parting guest*

A pair of lines which rhyme.

(i) extended metaphor

The image of the night dropping a veil and deliberately hiding the light.

Sometimes particular metaphors or images are carried through a poem and their force is thus increased by this extension.

**Poets and poetry**

Some well-known children's poets

Books of poetry you might have suggested are given next to each poet's name.

| | |
|---|---|
| John Agard | *Standing on a Strawberry* |
| Allan Ahlberg | *Please Mrs Butler* |
| Ted Hughes | *Season Songs* |
| Roger McGough | *In the Glassroom* |
| Eve Merriam | *There is no Rhyme for Silver* |
| Mary O'Neill | *Halibuts and Herring Bones* |
| Gareth Owen | *Salford Road* |
| Brian Patten | *Gargling Jelly* |
| Michael Rosen | *Mind Your Own Business* |
| Shel Silverstein | *Where the Sidewalk Ends* |
| Kit Wright | *Rabbiting on* |

Some of these poets are American. Their books are not as easy to obtain in this country as one would like, but worth hunting down.

You should be able to suggest many more than three poems for each of these poets.

**Forms of poetry**

Some poetic forms

Poem A is a couplet.

A couplet is a couple, or pair, of lines of poetry, usually rhymed. Sometimes the couplet stands by itself as a two-line poem, as in the example given. At other times longer poems are composed of sequences of couplets. A couplet is also sometimes used to summarize or complete a longer poem. Several of Shakespeare's sonnets use this device, including that used in this section.

Poem B is a limerick.

A limerick is a five-line poem, often humorous, in which lines 1, 2 and 5 contain three beats and rhyme, and lines 3 and 4 contain two beats and rhyme. Edward Lear is perhaps the best-known author of limericks and the example given is one of his.

An excellent series of books which contain many ideas for teaching children several of these forms are those by Sandy Brownjohn, published by Hodder & Stoughton.

Poem C is a sonnet.

A sonnet is a fourteen-line poem in which a single idea is set up, developed and brought to a conclusion at the end of the poem. Sonnets are often written on the subject of love or philosophy and are reflective pieces rather than action poems. Shakespeare is probably the best-known writer of sonnets in English and the example is from him.

Poem D is an acrostic.

An acrostic is a poem in which the first letters of the lines, read downwards, form a word, phrase or sentence. It is often thought of as a trivial form of poetry but has been used by many renowned poets such as Chaucer, Ben Jonson and Edgar Allan Poe. Some of the biblical Psalms are acrostics in the original Hebrew.

Poem E is a haiku.

A haiku is a form originating in Japan in which the poet tries to capture the essence of a particular moment, usually involving natural objects. In form it is three short lines. It is sometimes thought to have a strict syllable count of 5/7/5 in each line, but in practice this is not necessary.

### Looking at bias in text

It is fairly clear that the writer of the first account favours the voortrekkers in his/her telling of these events.

Phrases such as 'Matabele hordes', 'drinking the raw blood' and 'a savage attack' suggest a very negative image of the Matabele. On the other side the fact that the voortrekkers pray, help each other and, finally, give thanks to God suggest positive features.

From this account, ending as it does with the Matabele fleeing 'with their tails between their legs', it appears that the voortrekkers were the victors.

In the second account the two sides are portrayed differently. One side is referred to as the Ndebele, much closer to this group's own pronunciation of their name; these people are attacked first by the Boers before retaliating; and they are beaten off because of the Boers' superior firepower (presumably the Ndebele did not have guns).

In this account the outcome of the battle is not so clear cut. The Ndebele were beaten off, but not until they had killed all the Boers' sheep and cattle. Presumably it would be almost impossible for the trekkers to survive in difficult country without their supplies so the Ndebele may have felt they had done enough to drive off these invaders.

From the two accounts all we can reasonably conclude is that there was a clash between these two groups, the Boers had guns which helped in their defence, and they survived but at a heavy cost.

Some language features which affect a reader's response to a purportedly factual text include:
- choice of vocabulary to describe participants
- use of verbs and verb phrases to describe actions

*What makes a biased text?*

*There is no such thing as an unbiased text.*

*Language features affecting response*

Bear in mind that neither of these texts is unbiased, each being written by someone with their own values and attitudes.

It is useful to discuss these features with children.

- selection of events to report
- order in which events are reported

**Linguistic features at the text, sentence and word levels**

## Using texts to teach linguistic features

Some of the linguistic features you might have identified include the following:

(a) whole text level
  - written as narrative
  - written in the past tense
  - written in first person singular
  - autobiographical, from the narrator's point of view
  - informal style
  - changes of pace for effect, e.g. short sentences to emphasize points
  - attempt to engage reader: *And do you know ...*

> Although the features are listed here at the three levels, that does not imply that the best way to teach them is to separate the levels entirely. The best teaching is that which encourages children to make connections between the levels.

(b) sentence level
  - use of questions
  - use of exclamations
  - use of *and* to begin a sentence
  - use of metaphor, *my eyes on stalks*
  - different use of tense, *I shouted / She'd had her friends round*
  - direct speech

(c) word level
  - use of suffixes, e.g. *running*
  - use of prefix, e.g. *resolution*
  - use of simile, *like a battlefield*
  - compound words, e.g. *battle-field*
  - use of reference, e.g. *if **that** was what having friends round meant*
  - use of pronouns, e.g. *her friends*
  - noun phrases, e.g. *The bedclothes strewn across the floor*
  - definite/indefinite articles, e.g. *the scene, a battlefield*
  - verb forms, e.g. *shouted, was enjoying*

**Readability features**

## Looking at text difficulty

Features which can affect how difficult a text is to read include:

- how familiar a reader is with the content of the text
- the reader's previous experience of texts written like this, or on a similar topic
- the way the text is laid out on the page
- the amount of text on a page
- the length and format of the paragraphs in the text
- the physical size of the text
- the typeface used
- length of the sentences
- complexity of the sentences
- use of punctuation
- technical vocabulary
- presence of names of places, people, etc.
- word length and complexity

> How many of these features can you as a teacher control in any way?

# Textual structure and conventions

**What makes a narrative?**

## Looking at narrative

(a) The following language features characterize narrative:
- use of past tense, e.g. *pulled*, *stopped*
- a sequence of events
- predominant use of temporal connectives, e.g. *then*, *now*, *soon*

(b) The train text could not be satisfactorily described as a story.

**Characters, plot, resolution**

(c) It lacks a number of features:
- characters with whom readers can identify and empathize
- a structure beyond a simple list of events, that is, it has no beginning, middle or end
- a plot. Story plots usually involve the main characters trying to resolve some kind of problem; there is no problem here
- a resolution which provides the conclusion to the plot
- ingredients such as suspense, excitement, pathos, humour and so on

> Talking about these features with children may help them improve their own writing of stories as well as their appreciation of others' stories.

**Analysing stories**

## Story structure
The grid has been completed for the two fairy stories suggested as an example of how to analyse a story.

| STORY 1 | |
| --- | --- |
| The title of the story | *Red Riding Hood* |
| What is the setting of the story? | *A forest*<br><br>*Red Riding Hood's cottage*<br><br>*Grandmother's cottage* |
| List the main characters in the story. | *Red Riding Hood, her mother, her grandmother, the wolf, a woodcutter* |
| Sketch out the main events in the story. | *Red Riding Hood takes food to her grandmother.*<br><br>*Meets wolf on way.*<br><br>*He runs ahead and eats grandmother.*<br><br>*He pretends to be grandmother and plans to eat Red Riding Hood.*<br><br>*Red Riding Hood is saved by the woodcutter.* |
| What is the main problem faced by the characters in the story? | *How can Red Riding Hood avoid being eaten?* |
| How is this problem resolved? | *The woodcutter comes to the rescue and kills the wolf.* |

| STORY 2 | |
|---|---|
| The title of the story | *Sleeping Beauty* |
| What is the setting of the story? | *A castle* |
| List the main characters in the story. | *A king and queen, their daughter, a wicked witch, a prince* |
| Sketch out the main events in the story. | *The king and queen have a daughter.*<br><br>*They have a celebration but forget to invite the wicked witch.*<br><br>*She curses the daughter to prick her finger and fall asleep for 100 years.*<br><br>*The king and queen try to protect their daughter but to no avail.*<br><br>*She, and all the kingdom, fall asleep and huge thorns grow around the castle.*<br><br>*A prince finally comes and wakens Sleeping Beauty with a kiss.*<br><br>*They marry and everyone lives happily ever after.* |
| What is the main problem faced by the characters in the story? | *How can Sleeping Beauty be saved from the curse?* |
| How is this problem resolved? | *The prince rescues her and they marry.* |

## Looking at non-fiction texts

Text A is a discussion. Its purpose is to debate two contrasting positions and to reach a conclusion.

Text B is a recount. Its purpose is to give an account of a sequence of events.

Text C is a set of instructions. Its purpose is to give a set of directions which a reader can carry out to achieve a particular goal.

Text D is a report. Its purpose is to describe and present some facts about an object or group of objects.

Text E is an explanation. Its purpose is to advance a set of reasons underpinning a phenomenon.

Text F is persuasive writing. Its purpose is to convince a reader of a particular case.

The structural and language features of these texts are shown in the tables on the following pages.

Non-fiction genres

How much experience have you provided for pupils you have taught in writing each of these kinds of texts?

One very successful approach to teaching these kinds of texts is to use writing frames. (See Lewis, M. & Wray, D. (1996), *Developing Children's Non-fiction Writing*, Scholastic.)

| TEXT A | STRUCTURAL FEATURES |
|---|---|
| *The issue I would like to discuss is ...* | Opens with a statement of the issue to be discussed. |
| *Some people think that smoking is ...* | A list of points in favour of the issue is presented. |
| *Other people think that ...* | Followed by a list of points against the issue. |
| *I think that ...* | The writing concludes with a recommendation. |
| **LANGUAGE FEATURES** | • Generic participants – *some people, children.*<br>• Logical, not chronological, connectives – *so that, but, if.*<br>• Present tense used. |

| TEXT B | STRUCTURAL FEATURES |
|---|---|
| *OUR TRIP TO EXETER MUSEUM*<br>*On Tuesday ...* | Opens with an orientation to the topic of the recount. |
| *First of all we ...* | A list of events is given. |
| *It was a good trip. I ...* | The text concludes with a reorientation to the topic and a comment. |
| **LANGUAGE FEATURES** | • Personal participants – *we, my group.*<br>• Chronological connectives – *then, first.*<br>• Past tense used. |

| TEXT C | STRUCTURAL FEATURES |
|---|---|
| *OBJECT OF GAME*<br>*The object of the game is ...* | Opens with a statement of the goal of these instructions. |
| *EQUIPMENT*<br>*For the game you will need ...* | A list of equipment needed (ingredients) is given. |
| *HOW TO PLAY*<br>*1. Each player ...* | A list of steps to achieve the goal. |
| **LANGUAGE FEATURES** | • Generic participants – *you, each player.*<br>• Chronological and conditional connectives – *after, if.*<br>• Imperative used. |

| TEXT D | STRUCTURAL FEATURES |
|---|---|
| *LUNGS*<br>*Our lungs are ...* | Opens with a general classifying statement about the topic of the report. |
| *The lungs are divided ...* | A description of the phenomenon. |
| **LANGUAGE FEATURES** | • Generic participants – *lungs, we.*<br>• Conditional and logical connectives – *when, so.*<br>• Present tense used. |

| TEXT E | STRUCTURAL FEATURES |
|---|---|
| *THE WATER CYCLE*<br>*The water cycle is ...* | Opens with a general statement about the phenomenon to be explained. |
| *To begin with the sun shines ...* | A series of steps explaining the phenomenon. |
| **LANGUAGE FEATURES** | • Generic participants – *the sun, rain.*<br>• Chronological connectives – *next, finally.* (Logical connectives are also often used, although not in this case.)<br>• Present tense used. |

| TEXT F | STRUCTURAL FEATURES |
|---|---|
| *I think that ...* | Opens with a statement of the point of view to which the writer will try to persuade the reader. |
| *My first reason is that ...* | A number of points are put forward in the argument. Each point is elaborated upon. |
| *Therefore although some people think ...* | Concludes with a reiteration of the thesis of the text. |
| **LANGUAGE FEATURES** | • Generic participants – *wildlife, some people.*<br>• Logical connectives – *therefore, because.*<br>• Present tense used. |

**Paragraphs and topic sentences**

### Paragraphs

The original paragraph splits, and the reasons for them, were as follows (topic sentences in each paragraph are in bold type):

*Dinosaurs were the biggest animals that ever lived. They walked the earth many millions of years ago but are now extinct.* **Yet scientists know quite a lot about dinosaurs, including what they looked like and even what they ate.** *How do scientists know these things?*

This paragraph introduces the text and ends with a statement of the major theme.

**The main sources of information about dinosaurs are the fossilized remains which have been found in many parts of the world.** *Some of the very first dinosaur fossils to be uncovered were found in Britain in the cliffs at Lyme Regis. They were found by a local collector, Mary Anning.*

Some information is given about part of the theme before the text shifts topic to the major theme.

**From examining dinosaur fossils scientists have been able to work out a lot about the dinosaurs themselves.** *Some fossil skeletons, for example, have very big hind legs but tiny fore legs. This suggests that these dinosaurs must have walked on their hind legs only. Some fossil skeletons have very large sharp teeth. In others the teeth are smaller and less sharp. From this scientists can work out what these dinosaurs probably ate and whether they were meat eaters or plant eaters.*

Textual cohesion

### Textual cohesion

- *which* refers to *shine* earlier in the sentence
- *they* refers to *seekers*
- *Those* refers back to *seekers*
- *They* refers back to *seekers*

It would be fairly easy for young readers to read *Those wanting guidance* as referring back to the priests and priestesses as these were most recently mentioned.

> Research suggests that lack of awareness of cohesion in written text is one of the main factors which holds children back from making progress in their reading, especially at the late primary and early secondary stages.

Cohesive ties

### Cohesive ties

Text A includes an example of a lexical cohesive tie, more particularly a reiteration, i.e. repetition of the linking word *milk*.

Text B includes an example of a reference tie, in this case a personal reference as *her* refers back to *Queen*.

The tie in Text C is a demonstrative reference. This stands in place of the earlier clause.

Text D is an example of ellipsis. *Some* refers back to *bits of stone* but omits the *of them* qualifier used earlier.

Text E contains a substitution tie as *ones* is substituted for the earlier noun.

In Text F *it was* is elliptical, referring back to a much longer clause without repeating it.

In Text G *so* substitutes for what the headteacher said.

The tie in Text H is of the conjunction group. *For* joins together and defines the relationship in meaning between the two sentences.

Text I contains a lexical tie, using the familiar collocation of *fish* and *chips* to support its meaning.

Text J contains another example of a conjunction tie, with *then* signalling a temporal relationship between the two sentences.

Connectives

### Connectives

(a) **This** *was what he was holding: a large pistol pointed in my direction.*
   *This* is a cataphoric connective.

(b) *He said he liked rowing and that* **this** *was because of his schooldays.*
   *This* is an anaphoric connective.

(c) *Peter liked bread and jam* **but** *James would only eat plain bread.*
   *But* is a contradictive connective.

(d) *At the same time the Indians were circling the wagons yelling and whooping.*
   *At the same time* is a temporal connective.

(e) *John was similarly unhappy about the way events were unfolding.*
   *Similarly* is an addition connective.

(f) *Behind that wall, Peter knew, a dozen armed men were waiting expectantly.*
   *Behind that wall* is a spatial connective.

> In cataphora, the reference is forwards – you have to look ahead of the word to see what it is referring to. In anaphora, the reference is the other way – you need to look back to find it.

(g) *Thanks to John's foresight, nobody was hurt during the difficult crossing.*
*Thanks to* is a result connective.

(h) *Billy certainly did not like the experience, that is to say, he absolutely hated it.*
*That is to say* is an exemplification connective.

## Grammar and punctuation

### Parts of speech

Parts of speech

(a) adjectives:    *long* (line 1), *scattered* (5), *evident* (11), *impossible* (12)

    adverbs:     *up* (5), *together* (5), *open* (9), *still* (19), *there* (19)

    verbs:     *considered* (4), *absolved* (4), *hung* (9), *had contemplated* (16), *returned* (19), *was lying* (19)

    conjunctions: *and* (5), *and* (17)

    pronouns:     *I* (1), *she* (1), *they* (1), *I* (8), *you* (8), *she* (8), *him* (8), *she* (15), *this* (15), *those* (15), *she* (15), *her* (24)

(b) line 1:   *I, she, they*
    line 2:   *It*
    line 3:   *I, my, He, She*
    line 4:   *him*
    line 5:   *She, her*
    line 6:   *her, Her*
    line 7:   —
    line 8:   *I, it, you, she, him*
    line 9:   *her, his*
    line 10: *You, you, he*

(c) *Tom, Dick, Harry*
Proper nouns are the names of people, places, special events, etc. Other nouns are referred to as common nouns.

(d) *up, in, from, to, of, in*
Prepositions indicate position. They usually occur before a noun or a pronoun.

(e) *satisfaction, truth, presence, failure, pain, contempt* (abstract nouns)
Abstract nouns name things which cannot be touched, seen, tasted, heard or smelt. These include feelings, ideas and states.

    *sun, lunch, sandals, shirt, person, shoes* (concrete nouns)
Concrete nouns name things which can be touched, seen, tasted, heard or smelt.

(f) Transitive verbs are those which take a direct object, for example, 'The man hit the dog.' *Hit* is transitive. Intransitive verbs do not take a direct object. Thus in 'she stood up in the glare', *stood* is intransitive.

    *lying* (line 1) is intransitive.
    *ached* (line 6) is intransitive.
    *touched* (line 8) is transitive.
    *opening* (line 11) is transitive.
    *returned* (line 19) is intransitive.
    *made* (line 21) is transitive.

(g) *were lying* (line 1) is the past continuous tense, i.e. the event happened in the past but went on for a long time.

*considered* (line 4) is the past tense, i.e. it was completed in the past.

*won't be able* (line 10) is the future tense, i.e. the event will (or will not) happen in the future.

*I'm going* (line 18) is the present continuous tense, i.e. the event is currently happening.

*had sat* (line 24) is the pluperfect tense, i.e. it was in the past when the events in the passage were happening.

**Clauses and phrases**

### Looking at clauses and phrases

(a) *They were lying in the long grass* (lines 1–2) is a clause.

*that the sun absolved him* (line 4) is a clause.

*on the other side of town* (line 13) is a phrase.

*When she returned* (line 19) is a clause.

*in this venture* (line 15) is a phrase.

*to the back of her skull* (lines 17–18) is a phrase.

> These are the basic building blocks of the English sentence. A full description of how they work is given on pp.66–76 in *Developing your knowledge*.

(b) A clause contains a verb and could stand alone in terms of meaning. A phrase does not usually contain a verb and does not make sense by itself. The exception to this rule about containing verbs is the verb phrase: this is a group of words which acts as the verb in a sentence. Thus, in the sentence, He **quickly pushed open** the door, the highlighted group of words form a verb phrase.

(c) *She considered* (main clause) *that the sun absolved him* (subordinate clause)

*touched him with her foot* (main clause) *where his shirt hung open* (subordinate clause)

*She tried to persuade herself* (main clause) *that she wasn't as convinced of failure in this venture* (subordinate clause)

**Main and subordinate clauses**

The main clause contains the principal message of the sentence. Subordinate clauses qualify or limit the meaning of the main clause.

(d) *They were lying in the long grass in the field behind the house*
This is one clause.

*She sat up and began to gather together her scattered sandals and clothes and the remains of her lunch*
This contains two main clauses joined by the conjunction *and*.

*You won't be able to get up on time if you do*
This contains two clauses, a main clause (*You won't be able to get up on time*) and a subordinate clause (*if you do*).

*spreading his hot smile of contempt over the question as the heat of the day had sat upon her will*
This contains two clauses, a main clause (*spreading his hot smile of contempt over the question*) and a subordinate clause (as *the heat of the day had sat upon her will*).

(e) an adjective phrase in line 2: *behind the house*
a noun phrase in line 5: *her scattered sandals*
a verb phrase in line 5: *began to gather together*

an adverb phrase in line 6: *from the sun (and the wine)*
an adjective phrase in line 17: *from the grass*
a noun phrase in line 23: *his hot smile of contempt*
a verb phrase in line 19: *was still lying*

**Sentence types**

- statement:     e.g. *The man threw the bottle over the cliff.*
- question:      e.g. *Why did you do that?*
- command:       e.g. *Don't ever do that again.*
- exclamation:  e.g. *I will not be ordered about!*

Statements are usually direct descriptions of states of affairs. Most common is the straightforward Subject, Verb, Object sentence as in, *The dog bit the man*. Other variants are Subject Verb (*The dog died*), and Subject, Verb, Indirect object (*The dog went to heaven*). Statements can also be written in what is termed the Passive mode, as in, *The man was bitten by the dog*.

Questions are distinguishable by either their reversal of the normal Subject-Verb order or their use of auxiliary verb parts to break up the Subject-Verb link. So the statement *I am certain* becomes the question *Am I certain?* by the reversal of the Subject-Verb order. The statement *The dog bit the man* is changed to a question by the use of the auxiliary *did – Did the dog bite the man?* (Notice here that *bit* becomes *bite*. This is because the past tense form using the auxiliary *did* is *did bite*.)

Commands are indicated by their use of the imperative verb mode, thus *do this*, *get that*. Often the verb is placed at the beginning of the sentence in commands.

Exclamations are simply statements made with more force. Many exclamations consist of very short sentences, e.g. *Gosh!*, *Hurrah!*

**Punctuation**

(a) *Dr. Gregory rushed round to the house as quickly as she could.*
The full stop in *Dr.* indicates that this is an abbreviated form. The full stop at the end of the sentence indicates the end of that meaningful unit of language.

(b) *B.C.* and *a.m.* are abbreviations which are still pronounced as individual letters. Omitting the full stops would lead to confusion over how these should be pronounced.

*NATO* and *WRAF* are abbreviations that have graduated to become acronyms, that is words in their own right. To use the full stops would now be considered pedantic.

(c) *"I think that's true but then again ..." replied the chief in a puzzled voice.*
The three full stops in the middle of this sentence mark an ellipsis, that is a point at which something has deliberately not been said. Three full stops like this can also be used in transcriptions of spoken language to indicate pauses.

(d) *When I go fishing I use worms, bread, flies and maggots for bait.*
The commas separate words in a list or series. Note that the series is

*(sidebar)*
Sentence types and their language features

Full stops

Commas

concluded by *and* and therefore needs no comma between the two final items.

*Worms, especially the smaller ones, make wonderful bait.*
The commas enclose an explanatory phrase which qualifies the initial noun. The technical term is a phrase in apposition to the noun.

*Large, wriggly, fat earthworms do not make good bait.*
Commas are used to separate co-ordinate adjectives; adjectives which equally describe the same noun.

*If you cannot find the smaller worms, then maggots are the next best bet.*
Commas are used to separate an adverbial clause from the independent clause which follows it.

*Maggots, which are usually white, wriggle and attract the fish very well.*
Commas are used to enclose non-restrictive phrases or clauses, that is phrases or clauses which are not essential to the basic meaning of the sentence.

*You can buy maggots from The Fishing Shop, 24 High Street, Anglertown.*
Commas separate items in an address.

*"Why," you may say, "would I need to go to that shop?"*
Commas are used to set off words in direct speech from the rest of the sentence. Notice the position of the commas here, that is, inside the speech marks at the end of a section of direct speech and outside the speech marks at the beginning of a section.

*I would reply, dear angler, that it is simply the best place.*
Here the commas separate a vocative (the name of or reference to the person spoken to) from the rest of the sentence.

*In my time I must have bought over 10,000 maggots there.*
Commas also distinguish the thousands (and millions) in numbers.

## (e) Capital letters

Capital letters

| CORRECTLY CAPITALIZED TEXT | REASONS FOR DECISIONS |
|---|---|
| [1]The [2]U.S.A. is an excellent destination for holidays. ([3]It is also becoming cheaper to get there from [4]Britain.) [5]Skiing is a very popular sport in the [6]North and the [7]West but if you go [8]south you will find the weather is too warm for snow. | [1] Beginning of a sentence. [2] The name of a country. [3] Beginning of a sentence, even though inside brackets. [4] Name of a country. [5] Beginning of a sentence. [6] This word is used here as a place. [7] This word is used here as a place. [8] Here the word is a direction not a place. |
| I went skiing in [9]Lake Tahoe with [10]Uncle Bill last year. [11]My [12]uncle had a fright when he almost fell into the [13]lake. [14]The [15]Canadian instructor had to make a rapid [16]U-turn to help him out of the crevasse he had fallen into. | [9] Name of a place. [10] Name of a person. [11] Beginning of a sentence [12] *Uncle* here is not part of a name. [13] *Lake* here is not a name. [14] Beginning of a sentence. [15] Nationalities are always capitalized. [16] The first part of this word is treated as an abbreviation. |
| [17]The event was reported in the [18]*Lake Tahoe Times* and several [19]times after that [20]Bill was stopped by interested readers. [21]Although [22]Uncle Bill has a [23]Ph.D. he says he felt very foolish. | [17] Beginning of a sentence. [18] A name. [19] *Times* here is not a name but a common noun. [20] Name of a person. [21] Beginning of a sentence. [22] Name of a person. [23] Abbreviations for titles are capitalized. |
| I said to him, "[24]You'll have to take more care in future." | [24] Beginning of a spoken sentence in directly quoted speech. |

**Colons and semi-colons**

(f) Sentence 1 should contain a colon. The colon here is used to introduce a list.

Sentence 2 should contain a colon. Here the colon is used to emphasize a phrase which adds impact to the sentence.

Sentence 3 should contain a semi-colon. The semi-colon is used to join two independent clauses which are not connected with a co-ordinating conjunction. *And* could be used instead of the semi-colon here.

> Common co-ordinating conjunctions are *and* and *but*.

Sentence 4 should contain a semi-colon. The semi-colon is used to separate two long independent but connected clauses. It could be replaced by a full stop here but this would lessen the connection between the two sentence parts.

**Quotation marks**

(g) *"I don't really know," he said, "whether this year's drought will lead to higher prices."*

*I am "firm", you are "stubborn", he is "pig-headed".*

*Before you get into this "to boldly go" stuff, let me warn you I'm a very nervous traveller.*

*The poem chosen for the class to study was "The Raven" by Edgar Allan Poe.*

*"Have you never read 'The Raven?'" I asked the children incredulously.*
N.B. Note the embedded quotation marks, single inside double.

> Things can get even worse than this. Look at the punctuation of the following: *The teacher said, "I asked my class, 'Have you never read "The Raven"?'"* Can you work out what is happening?

(h) Apostrophes 1

*Don't go too near the water.*
*I wonder if she'd mind getting that for me.*
*It's very unlikely that I will have the time in the next day or so.*
*Now you're sure we can't do anything else for you?*
*Shall we go to the fish'n'chip shop to get our lunch.*

**Apostrophes**

The apostrophe is used to indicate omission of a letter or a group of letters.

(i) Apostrophes 2

*John Lennon's assassination shocked the world.*
*Teachers' skills lie in being able to spot pupils' problems quickly and then do something about them.*
*Children's clothes are much cheaper than adults'.*
*This is clearly somebody's field that we are walking through.*
*The man was selling shoes, books and several of his daughter's unworn dresses.*

The apostrophe is used to indicate possession. Thus it is the assassination of John Lennon. When the possessor is singular, the apostrophe is placed before the final s. When the possessor is plural, the apostrophe usually goes after the final s. Note the case of children's, though.

> A good rule to apply is always to put the apostrophe straight after the possessor. In the phrase parents' evening, the evening belongs to more than one parent, thus the possessor is parents. The apostrophe goes after this. In children's work, the possessor is children, so the same rule applies.

(j) The apostrophes are not strictly necessary in any of these examples. They do not indicate omission of letters or possession. They are present to indicate plural forms of words which normally do not have one. Sir Ernest Gowers in *The Complete Plain Words* recommends that 'Unless the reader really needs help it should not be thrust upon him' and would support the use of the apostrophe with single letters (*Mind your p's and q's*) but not with words (*too many and's*). He does not mention the case of dates (*the 1960's*) but this is becoming increasingly normal usage.

**Dialect, accent and standard English**

Dialect, accent and standard English

(a) Dialect: a language variety distinguished by differences in grammar and vocabulary.

Accent: variety in the pronunciation of language.

Standard English: a dialect of English with high social status and wide currency.

> Note that just because someone speaks with a strong accent, this does not necessarily indicate he/she uses a dialect other than standard English. Accent is purely to do with pronunciation.

(b) In the passage the following features indicate dialect characteristics. Many of the features represent accent rather than any particular divergence from standard English grammar and/or vocabulary.

| | |
|---|---|
| *Ah's* | representing *I is*, the dialect form of the Standard English *I am*. |
| *agin* | a dialect form of *against*. |
| *yan* | a dialect form of *one*. |
| *missen* | a dialect form of *myself*. |
| *yance* | a dialect form of *once*. |
| *were* | a dialect form of the standard English *was*. |
| *wor* | a dialect form of *was*. |

With standard English grammar and vocabulary the passage would read:

> *"I'm not against dogs. I used to own one myself once. Her name was Jade, and she was a really grand dog. She used to take me for a walk every day without fail, rain or shine, whether I wanted to go out or not. To tell the truth, taking her out was a bit of a drag: she dragged me through bushes, hedges, trees, ponds – I just couldn't control her. When I was finally allowed to go back home – usually when she was feeling hungry – the neighbours had phoned the police. They thought I'd been mugged. They weren't far wrong, either."*

(c) This girl's use of grammar differs from standard English in the following ways:

Past tense represented by standard English present tense forms.

Omission of auxiliary verbs, that is, *Where you going* rather than *Where **are** you going ... ?*

Possession indicated differently – *grandmother house*.

(d) Dialect forms

- multiple negation:          e.g. *He didn't want none of it.*
- past tense verb forms:     e.g. *He come home yesterday.*
- relative pronouns:           e.g. *This is the man what said it.*
- demonstrative pronouns: e.g. *Them ones over there.*
- personal pronouns:         e.g. *Us don't like doing that.*
- forms of the verb 'to be': e.g. *You'm being really stupid.*

## How words work

**Phonology – the sound system of spoken words**

(a) The following words are segmented into syllables.

*bun/ga/low*     *win/dow*     *mag/ni/fi/cent*
*com/pu/ter*     *cha/ri/ty*

A syllable is the smallest unit of speech that consists of a vowel alone or a combination of consonants and vowels. You can use a number of ways to decide where to split words into syllables. One is to listen for the "beats".

(b) Stressed syllables are pronounced louder, longer or at a different pitch from unstressed syllables.

*<u>su</u>permarket*     *<u>mar</u>malade*     *se<u>crete</u>*
*<u>lo</u>nely*     *<u>bas</u>ket*     *re<u>fri</u>gerator*

(c) Placing the stress on certain syllables can affect the meaning of words. Heteronyms are words with the same spelling but a different meaning and pronunciation.

*<u>ob</u>ject (a thing)*     *<u>re</u>fuse (rubbish)*
*ob<u>ject</u> (to something)*     *re<u>fuse</u> (to do something)*
*com<u>bine</u> (to mix)*     *<u>re</u>ject (something cast aside)*
*<u>com</u>bine (a harvesting machine)*     *re<u>ject</u> (to cast something aside)*

(d) The schwa (unstressed vowel) sounds in unstressed syllables mean that it can be difficult to tell which unstressed vowel to write by listening to the word spoken.

*above*     *suppose*     *scenery*     *sofa*

(e) The onset sound is the sound at the beginning of the syllable. The rime is the sound made by the rest of the syllable, usually a vowel and consonant.

*string*: The onset sound is *str-*. The rime is *-ing*.
*zig/zag*: This word has two syllables. There is an onset sound and rime for each syllable. The onset sounds are both *z-* the rimes are *-ig* and *-ag*.
*cat*: The onset sound is *c-* the rime is *-at*.
*fire*: The onset sound is *f-* the rime is *-ire*.
*buil/ding*: This word has two syllables. There is an onset sound and rime for each syllable. In the first syllable the onset is *b-* and the rime *-uil*; in the second syllable, the onset is *d-* and the rime *-ing*.

(f) Some words which rhyme but have final syllables which are spelt differently include the following:

*views, choose* and *muse*
*pear, chair* and *stare*
*beat, mete* and *feet*
*no, sloe* and *dough*
*fire, higher* and *liar*

Syllables

Stressed and unstressed syllables

Heteronyms

Onset and rime sounds

Rhyming words

Note that this section is based upon the phonology of Received Pronunciation, being the most widely accepted English accent. There are many regional accents of English in which many of the points made here simply do not apply.

Words which share the same rime also rhyme.

(g) Words which rhyme when more than one of the final syllables sound the same include the following:

> *admiringly* and *conspiringly*
> *inspiring* and *retiring*
> *snigger* and *trigger*

(h) The 26 letters of the alphabet represent 44 phonemes (speech sounds). The 20 vowel phonemes (sounds) and 24 consonant phonemes (sounds) are listed on p.83 in *Developing your knowledge*.

(i) Some letter combinations in words represent phonemes.

> *dish*: /sh/ is one phoneme
> *walking*: /ng/ is one phoneme
> *choice*: /ch/ is one phoneme

**Analysing words into phonemes**

(j) How many speech sounds (phonemes) are there in the following words?

> *that*: 3
> *fisher*: 4
> *swing*: 4
> *mishap*: 6
> *apple*: 3

(k) Segment the following words into phonemes.

> *w/i/n/d/ow/*      *r/ea/d/y*      *ch/a/r/i/t/y*

**Blends, digraphs and trigraphs**

(l) Which of the phonemes highlighted in the words below are consonant blends and which are consonant digraphs or trigraphs?

| Consonant Blends | Consonant Digraphs | Consonant Trigraphs |
|---|---|---|
| *train* *split* | *shirt* *bring* *this* *chip* *where* | *match* *fright* |

> Blends occur when the two consonants keep their sounds. In digraphs, the two consonants make another sound entirely. In trigraphs this is achieved by three consonants.

**Long and short vowels**

(m) Long vowels make a longer sound than short vowels.

| Words containing short vowels | Words containing long vowels |
|---|---|
| *can* | *cane* |
| *bed* | *cede* |
| *rut* | *rude* |
| *hid* | *hide* |
| *rot* | *rote* |

The rule which applies to the pronunciation of the vowels underlined above is usually called the 'magic e' rule. When an <e> is added to a consonant vowel consonant (CVC) word, the first vowel is pronounced as a long vowel. Sometimes children are told that the magic <e> makes the first vowel say its name.

> However, note the exceptions: have, live, give, love and above.

**Digraphs and diphthongs**

(n) Two written letters which make a single vowel sound are called a vowel digraph. A diphthong is a vowel which makes two vowel sounds: it can be written as one or two letters. In the word *rain*, for example, the long *a* vowel is actually a combination of two vowel sounds – a short *e* followed by a long *e*.

| VOWEL DIGRAPHS | DIPHTHONGS | |
| --- | --- | --- |
| l*eo*pard | f*ai*l | t*oy* |
| br*ea*d | p*ai*n | l*eo*nine |
| sp*ee*ch | *ear* | br*oo*ch |
| | h*ei*ght | h*ear* |

Young children often go through a stage of spelling when they represent diphthongs as distinct letters, e.g. daey, niyt.

(o) The words below have an irregular sound-symbol correspondence because the letters do not represent the sounds in their normal way.

*bough:* the letters *ough* represent the same sound as /ow/ in *now*

*mention:* *tio* represents the same phoneme as /sh/ in *ship*

*balm:* the letter *l* is silent and lengthens the vowel phoneme represented by *a*

*tongue:* the letters *ongue* represent the same sounds as /u/n/g/ in *hung*

**Graphology – the alphabetic spelling system**

**Graphemes**

(a) The alphabet has 26 letters. Each of these is a grapheme.

(b) The five most frequently used letters in written English are <e> < t> <a > <o> and <i>. The least frequently used are <z> <q> <j> <x>and <k>.

This is not a terribly useful thing to know, unless you enjoy playing Hangman!

(c) Each grapheme can be represented by a number of different letter shapes (graphs). Different graphs for a letter include the different fonts or typefaces used in printing and the upper and lower case graphs for the graphemes. The <a> (or any other letter) remains the same letter whichever font it is written in.

(d) Words which include the long /e/ sound but do not represent it using <ee> include the following:

| *heat* | *beat* | *lead* |
| --- | --- | --- |
| *delete* | *cede* | |

(e) There are several spellings for these phonemes:

/a/ in *play, a, ape, ate, laid, late, paid*
/i/ in *line, malign, eye, sigh*
/ow/ in *cow, plough, count*
/er/ in *bird, hurt, learn, curtail*

(f) Some letter strings which are phonologically regular include:

-and *sand, hand, land, handle, candle, android, candy*
-ell *sell, bell, well, swell, hell, Wellington*
-ink *think, wink, pink, sinker, blink, drink, mink, inkwell*

There are many others including -ash, -ank, -ang, -ung, -end, -uck, -ock.

(g) Visually regular spelling strings may represent a number of phonemes. The following are some examples:

| | |
|---|---|
| -ough | *through, cough, bough, thought, thorough* |
| -or | *core, worm, orange* |
| -er | *error, erase, gripper* |
| -ear | *hearing, learning, wearing* |

**Silent letters**

(h) In English all the letters except for f, j, q, r and v may be unpronounced. The following are some examples.

b in *numb, lamb* and *comb*      n in *damn*
c in *scythe*      p in *psychology*
d in *handsome*      s in *island*
g in *foreign*      t in *hutch* and *match*
h in *honest* and *hotel*      w in *wrong* and *write*
(although pronunciation varies)      x in *prix*
k in *knee, knot* and *knickers*      y in *key*
l in *talk, palm* and *calm*      z in *laissez-faire*
m in *mnemonic*

**Homographs**

(i) Homographs are identical in spelling but different in meaning, origin and pronunciation. Examples include:

*entrance* (the way in)      *lead* (take, conduct, guide)
*entrance* (to put in a trance)      *lead* (a heavy metal)
*sow* (plant seeds)
*sow* (female pig)

**Morphology – word meanings, structure and derivations**

(a) The smallest units of meaning are called morphemes. A word may contain one or more morphemes.

*house-s:*   *House* is a single morpheme. The morpheme *-s* makes it plural.

*differ-ent:*   *Differ* is a single morpheme verb. The inflectional morpheme *-ent* makes it into an adjective.

*cat:*   A single morpheme as neither *c-* nor *-at* means anything on its own.

*skipp-ing:*   The single morpheme for the verb *skip* is transformed into a participle by the addition of the morpheme *-ing*.

*ed-ible:*   The stem morpheme *ed-* (related to *eat*) becomes an adjective through the addition of *-ible*.

*re-vis-ed:*   The three morphemes in this word are all commonly used in other combinations (*recapitulate, vision, jumped*).

**Stems, prefixes and suffixes**

(b) The stem is the basic meaning of a word. Prefixes are units of meaning added at the beginning of the word. Suffixes are units of meaning added at the end of the word.

| PREFIXES | STEM | SUFFIXES | |
|---|---|---|---|
| *un-* | faith | *-ful* | |
| *anti-* | perspir | *-ant* | |
| *un-* | different | *-iat* | *-ed* |
| *super-* | charg | *-ed* | |
| *in-* | appropriate | *-ness* | |
| *dis-* | appear | *-ance* | |

(c) Some meanings can be represented by a number of prefixes.

| PREFIX | MEANING | ORIGIN | ALTERNATIVES |
|---|---|---|---|
| *ante-* | before | Latin | *pre-* |
| *anti-* | opposite or against | Greek | *contra-* |
| *post-* | after | Latin | *after-* |
| *trans-* | across, through, beyond, over | Latin | *cross-* |
| *de-* | down, off, or the reverse or removal of a process | Latin | *un-* |
| *sub-* | under | Latin | *under-* |

This does not mean, however, that these prefixes are interchangeable. We would say inappropriate, not unappropriate, for instance.

(d) Inflectional suffixes change the grammatical status of a word.

| WORD | SUFFIX | NATURE OF CHANGE |
|---|---|---|
| cat | -s | singular to plural |
| baby (y changes to ie) | -s | singular to plural |
| jump | -ed | present to past tense |
| great | -est | superlative adjective |
| high | -er | comparative adjective |
| teacher | -'s | possessive |

Derivational suffixes create words in a new word class.

| WORD | WORD CLASS | SUFFIX | NEW WORD | NEW WORD CLASS |
|---|---|---|---|---|
| bare | adjective | -ly | barely | adverb |
| rational | adjective | -ize | rationalize | verb |
| promotion | noun | -al | promotional | adjective |

e) The inflectional suffixes change the grammatical status of each word.

| WORD | SUFFIX | EFFECT |
|---|---|---|
| frog | -s | singular to plural |
| be | -ing | present verb to participle |
| help | -ed | present tense to past tense |
| high | -est | superlative adjective |

(f) Derivational suffixes create words in a new word class.

| WORD | WORD CLASS | SUFFIX | NEW WORD | NEW WORD CLASS |
|---|---|---|---|---|
| rough | adjective | -en | roughen | verb |
| high | adjective | -ly | highly | adverb |
| fiction | noun | -al | fictional | adjective |
| rational | noun | -ize | rationalize | verb |

(g) The regular past tense uses an *-ed* suffix.

| PRESENT TENSE | PAST TENSE | CONVENTION OR RULE |
|---|---|---|
| rain<br>open | rained<br>opened | add *-ed* |
| bat<br>hop | batted<br>hopped | the suffix beginning in a vowel added to a word ending in a single vowel and consonant requires the consonant to double |
| need | needed | the suffix beginning in a vowel added to a word ending in a double vowel and consonant does not require the consonant to double |
| rebel<br>omit | rebelled<br>omitted | when the final vowel is stressed the final consonant is doubled |
| utter | uttered | when the final vowel is not stressed the final consonant is not doubled |
| hope<br>rate | hoped<br>rated | when the word ends in <e> the suffix *-d* is added |

(h) The usual way to form plurals in English is to add *-s* or *-es*.

| WORD | PLURAL | CONVENTION OR RULE |
|---|---|---|
| cat<br>frog | cats<br>frogs | when the word ends in a vowel and consonant add *-s* |
| inch<br>fish | inches<br>fishes | when the word ends in two consonant graphemes representing a consonant digraph add *-es* |
| half<br>calf | halves<br>calves | usually, the final *f* becomes *v* and *-es* is added, but remember *roofs* |
| baby<br>lady | babies<br>ladies | when a word ends in *-y* following a consonant the final *y* becomes *ie* and *-s* is added. |
| monkey<br>turkey | monkeys<br>turkeys | when a word ends in a vowel followed by *-y* add *-s* |
| potato<br>hero | potatoes<br>heroes | words ending in *-o* add *-es* |

## Words

**Homonyms**

(a) Homonyms are words which sound the same and look the same but have different meanings. Here are some examples.

*bill* (a statement of money owed)   *bear* (an animal)
*bill* (beak)   *bear* (to carry)
*cell* (in a prison)   *ear* (of corn)
*cell* (in a living organism)   *ear* (to hear with)

**Homophones**

(b) Homophones are words which sound the same but have a different form and meaning. Here are some examples.

*tale* (a story)   *blew* (the wind)
*tail* (of an animal)   *blue* (the colour)
*rowed* (a boat)   *bold* (brave)
*rode* (a horse)   *bowled* (a ball)

**Synonyms and antonyms**

(c) A synonym is a word or phrase with the same meaning. An antonym is a word or phrase with the opposite meaning. Here are some examples.

| WORD | SYNONYM | ANTONYM |
|---|---|---|
| nice<br>help<br>top | pleasant<br>aid<br>summit | nasty<br>hinder<br>bottom |

Word origins

(d) Compound words are made by putting two words together. Some examples include: *blackbird, headache, sleepwalk* and *shoelace*. Some compound words are written without a space between the elements (*scarecrow*); some are written with a hyphen between the elements (*chewing-gum, sea-green*); and some are written with a space between the elements (*gold mine*). In some cases the usage varies.

(e) Blend words are a type of abbreviation where a new word is made by combining bits of other words.

> *breakfast + lunch = brunch*
> *international + police = interpol*
> *news + broadcast = newscast*

(f) Words borrowed from other languages are known as borrowings. Borrowings in English reflect the history of the language.

| WORD | ORIGIN |
|---|---|
| *criterion* | Greek |
| *hammock* | Arawakan indian |
| *shampoo* | India (Hindi/Urdu) |
| *hooligan* | Irish |
| *coleslaw* | Dutch |
| *memorandum* | Latin |
| *ski* | Norwegian |

Some words which have come to English from Latin include the following.

| | | | |
|---|---|---|---|
| *bacteria* | *flora* | *medium* | *opera* |
| *cactus* | *fungus* | *memory* | *revise* |
| *data* | *literacy* | *noble* | *status* |

> In some of these words the Latin derivation is seen clearly when they are pluralized. Thus we get *cacti, fungi, media,* etc. which do not follow the normal English rules for plurals.

Some words which have come to English from French include the following.

| | | | |
|---|---|---|---|
| *allow* | *café* | *destroy* | *hostel* |
| *avant-garde* | *castle* | *forest* | *poison* |
| *beauty* | *conquest* | *garage* | *limousine* |

(g) Other terms for *daps* include:

| | |
|---|---|
| *sandshoes* | North East England |
| *plimsolls* | South East England |
| *pumps* | North West England |
| *galoshers* | South Cumbria |

## Looking at children's language

Word level

**Examining children's writing**

There are several levels at which you can comment upon each of the pieces of writing given. Here are some of the points you might have commented upon:

*At a sub-word or word level*
- Spelling errors

What kind of errors are these? Emily's spelling of *sprinckle* appears to be a phonological error (the letters she uses make the right sounds). Peter's spelling of *strats* seems, on the other hand to be a visual error. Peter makes several such errors (*ran, flot, thy*). He appears to be a visual speller. You might also notice that Melanie uses single consonants in place of double consonants consistently in two words (*ketle, glas*).

- Breadth and appropriateness of vocabulary
There is little difference on this criteria between all four pieces of writing, unless you count James' *planting plate* as a piece of technical vocabulary.

- Use of capitalization
Emily seems not to understand the rules for this, using capitals in the middle of sentences and lower case at the beginning.

**Sentence level**

*At a sentence level*
- Tense
Neither instructions nor explanations are written in the past tense. James and Melanie do not understand this. Emily and Peter, on the other hand, use an appropriate tense for the type of writing they are producing.

- Use of imperative/declarative verbs
Instructions are written in the imperative mode. Emily understands this, e.g. *get a plate*, whereas James uses declarative verbs only.

- Use of connectives
Explanations tend to use connectives other than chronological ones. Melanie uses only chronological connectives (*then* twice) in her explanation. Peter uses causal connectives (*because, so*) which are more appropriate to an explanation.

- Use of punctuation
Emily is the only child who uses punctuation other than full stops. Her use of commas in her first sentence suggests a fairly sophisticated understanding of sentence structure.

- Sentence structure
All the children use single clause sentences and compound sentences. There are some examples of complex sentences. Emily's first sentence shows understanding of how to use lists. Her final sentence contains two conditional clauses, *when it is 9cm long* and *when it is ready*. James uses predominantly compound sentences joined by *and* and *then*. His final sentence is, however, more complex and contains two linked adverbial clauses, *to see / if they have grown*.

**Text level**

*At a text level*
- Organization
Emily adopts the appropriate organizational pattern for her writing. She gives a list of ingredients, then a number of steps the reader should take to achieve the goal of growing the seeds. James does not do this, but instead narrates the story of how he planted seeds. Narration is also used by Melanie, whereas Peter does attempt a more general explanation of *why* the rain falls.

• Use of generic or personal participants

Neither instructions nor explanations will usually mention individual people. They will usually refer to generic participants: classes of things in explanations and a general implied reader in instructions. Emily and Peter achieve this. Emily mentions no participants at all and implies the *you*. Peter's participants are the generic *rain, water*, etc. James and Melanie, on the other hand, use the specific *we* as well as the names of particular people.

• Clarity and detail of the content

Emily gives all the details needed in a very clear way. James gives a lot of information but omits some crucial points. He does not mention adding water to the seeds and his point about checking the seeds to see if they have grown does not mention how he will know if they have grown enough. Both Peter and Melanie miss fairly important details from their accounts. Melanie does not attempt to explain why the phenomena she reports happened and Peter's explanation of the water getting hot and floating up to the sky is rather lacking in precision.

• Fitness for purpose/genre

Emily and Peter get fairly close to the genre they are supposed to be writing. James and Melanie write in the wrong genre, producing recounts rather than instructions or an explanation.

**Examining children's reading**

Here are some of the points you might have commented upon:

Diagnosing reading

*Reading aloud*

• Amount of pauses/fluency/number of words read correctly

There are fourteen longish pauses in Lisa's reading compared with only three in William's. This suggests that William is the more fluent reader of this passage. William reads ten words incorrectly (he self-corrects two of these), exactly the same number as Lisa, but, as we see later, there is a good deal of difference in the kinds of mistakes both children make.

• Use of initial sound cues

When Lisa comes to words she does not know she generally has a go at pronouncing them. In those she gets wrong, she appears to adopt the strategy of looking carefully at the initial letters, sounding these and then guessing the rest of the word from there. This is not a terribly successful strategy for her as it results in ten errors in word reading. William does not appear to be as fixated on a single strategy of guessing from the initial sounds. Seven of his nine word-reading errors do show the use of the initial letter sounds but in two of his errors (*houses* for *buildings*, *went* for *paraded*) he is clearly using a different strategy.

• Reading for understanding

William's reading shows an attempt to read for meaning. In every case, his errors do not significantly affect the meaning of the passage. In the two cases where he is clearly not using letter sounds as a basis for word attack (*houses* for *buildings*, *went* for *paraded*) his substitutions also make sense, which suggests he is trying to understand what he reads. Lisa, on the other hand, makes a number of errors which do not maintain the meaning of the passage. She clearly is not reading for understanding as what she reads does not make any real sense.

- Attending to syntax

Lisa's word substitutions are generally, but not infallibly, syntactically appropriate; only *ever* for *everyone* and *ball* for *brand* show a change of word class from the original words of the passage (it is impossible to decide this for her substitution of *pard* for *paraded*). There is sufficient disparity between the words she reads and the original words, however, to suggest that an awareness of syntax was not playing a large part in her reading. William does show such an awareness. All of his substitutions are of an appropriate word class and the one substitution he makes which does not maintain the precise form of the original word (*say* for *said*) is swiftly corrected. This reinforces the impression that William is reading using a range of cues and is actively monitoring the meanings he is creating as he reads.

- Self-correction

Lisa makes no self-corrections, whereas William makes two. He appears to be monitoring his reading of the passage and, probably, using more than one source of information to determine the words to be read. Lisa seems limited to one source of information only – initial sound cues.

*Comprehension*
- Sequence of events

Both readers retell the events of the passage in an appropriate order, although Lisa's order is not strictly that of the passage. She begins with a piece of information not mentioned until near the end of the passage (*He was ... grand*). She also leaves a statement of why the people were looking at the King (*to see his clothes*) until near the end of her retelling, whereas this figures early on in the original passage.

- Relative importance of events

Both children mention most of the crucial events of the passage, although only William gets the point of the spectators in the passage being silent (he also tries to offer an explanation). Lisa says that *they were all cheering*, which is the opposite of what it says in the text.

- Degree of detail

William is able to give many more details in his retelling, enlivening it with ideas of his own. He also, unlike Lisa, is able to provide a motivation for the described events beyond that explicitly mentioned in the passage.

- Prediction

Lisa can make no predictions from the text, even when she is specifically asked to. William, on the other hand, has clearly engaged with the passage to such an extent that he is able to go beyond it and to make sensible suggestions about where the story might lead.

- Enjoyment

In making his predictions, William is clearly responding to the passage with some enthusiasm, even laughing aloud as he considers the events of the story. Lisa shows little sign of enjoying what she has read, or of responding personally to it.

- Use of vocabulary from the passage

Both children use some vocabulary from the passage as they read it. Lisa could not read several of the words so therefore did not have them available to use in her retelling. William includes in his retelling a word (*clambered*) which is only there because he misread it for *climbed*.

*Summary*

These children are very different readers. They have different strategies for decoding text, with Lisa seemingly locked into using initial sound cues as her chief decoding strategy. William uses a wider range of strategies, responding to meaning as well as sounds, and shows evidence of active monitoring of his own reading. Lisa does not show such monitoring here, but this was a difficult task for her as the passage was clearly too hard for her to read comfortably.

Because the task of decoding this text was so difficult for Lisa, she appears to have had little cognitive capacity left to make real sense of what she has read. Given this it is, perhaps, unsurprising that she is unable to really enjoy the text she has read. William, by comparison, is able to respond much more extensively to the text, predicting, bringing to bear his previous knowledge and generally enjoying the experience.

# Developing your knowledge

The importance of a knowledge of children's literature

**Developing your knowledge of children's literature**

Most definitions of literacy go beyond the merely functional ability to read and write to include some indication that what one reads and writes is also important. Were we to produce children from our schools who could read but only ever did so when they had an immediately pressing need such as to catch a bus, most teachers would feel that they had failed to some degree to make these children literate. Teachers have the feeling that to produce literate children they need to introduce those children to a range of texts which will capture their imaginations and make them want to read. Of course, in order to do this teachers need themselves to have an extensive knowledge of children's literature.

How can you develop this knowledge? It has been estimated that around 5000 new children's books are published annually, and this does not take into account new editions of books previously published. How can you possibly keep up to date? How can you approach the problem of ensuring range?

Categories of children's books

One approach is to categorize the books we make available to children. There are several categorizations you might find useful. One is to think about the types of books we should provide. Primary schools might, for example, try to get a good supply of:

- picture books for younger children. These make an obvious contribution to the reading of young children, being very visually attractive and usually having few words to read. Authors such as Eric Carle, Pat Hutchins, Jan Ormerod, Shigeo Watanabe, Janet and Allan Ahlberg, Ruth Brown, and David McKee should feature in any reasonable collection.

Quality in children's literature

- picture books for older children. Picture books are not just for early readers and there are several excellent books aimed at much more sophisticated readers. Authors such as Victor Ambrus, Anthony Browne, Graham Oakley, Philippe Dupasquier, John Burningham, Nina Sowter and Jez Alborough have produced several books which even teenagers can find intriguing.

- cartoon books. Many reluctant readers, especially boys, can be switched on to reading through cartoon books. These can be surprisingly demanding, as, for example, in the pun-rich *Astérix* books. Indeed, in France, such books, (*bandes dessinés*), are among the most widely read adult fiction titles.

---

The difference implied here is often characterized as teaching children to read versus helping children become readers. Of course, the real aim is to do both of these.

You might look on this 'problem' as an opportunity. As a teacher, you can legitimately immerse yourself in children's literature. Most people would love to do this, but cannot justify the time it takes. You can – it's your professional duty!

Look at Philippe Dupasquier's *Dear Daddy*, for example. Here you have a book with three stories taking place at the same time. Holding each of these in your mind and making the necessary links between them is quite challenging. Authors like Anthony Browne make even greater demands upon their readers through the detailed allusions and jokes contained in the illustrations.

- pop-up books. Pop-up and lift-the-flap books have become immensely popular over the last few years and children generally love them. Jan Pienkowski's books are brilliantly engineered and designed, while at a simpler level, Eric Hill's *Spot* books are widely loved.

- collections of short stories. Many children will prefer books with several short stories to one long continuous text.

- myths, legends and folktales. There are many versions available of the familiar Greek, Roman and Norse legends and myths. These will appeal to children at Key Stage 2. Authors to look for include Roger Lancelyn Green, Rosemary Sutcliff and Henry Treece.

- longer novels. Children also need books to become absorbed in and there are a vast number at all reading levels, from Florence Parry Heide's stories about *Treehorn*, to Leon Garfield's historical novels.

You might also categorize children's literature by genre, i.e. adventure stories, science fiction, school stories, stories about animals, etc. This can sometimes be useful but often individual books will seem to cross these boundaries. *Mrs Frisby and the Rats of Nimh*, for example, is about animals but it is also an adventure and a fantasy.

Quality will also be a consideration in your selection of books for children. All things being equal, teachers would always say they wanted to make available the best possible books to their children. Yet quality in literature can be a difficult thing to ascertain. Authors such as Enid Blyton and Roald Dahl are extremely popular with young children, yet many adults would question the quality of their work. Blyton particularly has been described as merely a hack writer with very few original ideas. You will need to decide whether you would include such authors in your classroom collection, and on what grounds you would either include or not include them.

One argument might be that it is unrealistic to expect children to read only high quality literature. This is not, after all, what adults do (otherwise Dick Francis and Jeffrey Archer would not be so popular!). A mixture in quality might be more reasonable for children.

**Representation in children's books**

One aspect of book choice you will certainly want to consider is that of representation. How do the books you make available for children represent social, gender and cultural differences? A great deal has been written about the problems of racism and sexism in children's books. Again, the only person who can decide what is appropriate for your children is you, bearing in mind their backgrounds, current interests and prejudices. Yet it is to be hoped that one of the criteria for a collection of children's literature is that it should fairly represent the nature of the society in which we live, and should not perpetuate the negative features of that society. If books such as *Doctor Dolittle* (racist) and *The Famous Five* (sexist) are still felt worthy of a place on the classroom shelves, then they should be balanced by books which give other, contrasting messages.

**Help with book selection**

Book selection is not a simple task. Who might you approach for help? There are a number of people/places to be aware of:

- local libraries and librarians. Probably the first place to visit. Many local libraries have children's librarians who are very knowledgeable about children's books and who can make suggestions. You will also be able to view the books before buying them.

---

You might find, as I did, that Bill Naughton's *The Goalkeeper's Revenge* is the collection which transforms the reading habits of some older boys. George Layton has also produced several collections of stories along these lines (e.g. *The Fib*, *The Balaclava Boys*).

One genre currently extremely popular among children is the horror story. R.L.Stine is the best-known author here.

Enid Blyton's books are also variously condemned as sexist, racist (think of that naughty golliwog!) and class-biased. Yet generations of children have lapped them up.

We should also question just how we arrive at definitions of 'quality' in children's literature. This must inevitably involve subjective judgements.

Many people will say, of course, that reading books such as *Doctor Dolittle* 'never did me any harm'. There are two points to make here. Firstly, they may have done some people harm – people who felt belittled by their caricatures of other races. Secondly, we do not always know what effect a book is having on us. The fact that it makes racial stereotyping possible may be harm enough.

- professional development centres. In some areas the local Teachers' or Professional Development Centre will hold a collection of up-to-date and recommended children's books. Sometimes the centre, or the local School Library Service, will offer a loan service. If this is the case, use it.

- publishers. Publishers will always supply you with their latest catalogues and sometimes allow you to receive books on an inspection copy basis, to return (undamaged) if you find they are not suitable.

- booksellers. Local bookshops can also be very helpful places to visit. One very successful scheme I ran once involved taking my class for a visit to the local bookshop where each child was asked to select and recommend one book they thought the rest of the class would like to read. When the books arrived in school they were marked as 'Selected by [child's name] for the use of Class 5'.

> Bookshops will also sometimes let you have promotional material such as posters, which you can then display in your classroom.

- journals/magazines. A number of magazines specialize in children's books and provide information and reviews of the latest publications. You would find a subscription to one of *Books for Keeps*, *Books for Your Children*, *Growing Point* or the *School Librarian* extremely useful as a way of keeping up to date.

**Children's book awards**

- book awards. A number of annual awards for children's books provide together an excellent indication of quality in new literature. The best known are:

> The Carnegie Medal for an outstanding children's book.
> The Kate Greenaway Medal for distinguished children's book illustration.
> The Guardian Award for children's fiction.
> The Kurt Maschler Award for excellent integration of text and illustration.
> The Mother Goose Award for the best newcomer to children's book illustration.
> The Children's Book Award for fiction for children up to fourteen.
> The Whitbread Literary Award for the best novel for children aged over seven.
> The Other Award for progressive anti-racist, anti-sexist literature.
> The Young Observer Teenage Fiction Award for a teenage novel.

### Developing a knowledge of poetry for children

In the same way that a knowledge of children's literature is important in the effective teaching of literacy, a knowledge of poetry for children is also a valuable part of the teacher's armoury of knowledge. The case of poetry is somewhat special, however, since the evidence suggests that it tends to be neglected in schools. Reports have suggested that young children are given infrequent opportunities to hear poetry read aloud or to read it for themselves: much of children's experience with poetry seems to occur when it is used as source material for comprehension lessons or handwriting practice.

**The benefits of poetry**

Despite this gloomy picture, it is still true that poetry has several potential benefits for the development of children's literacy.

- It can motivate children to read if it is treated as a source of pleasure.

- It can foster improved listening in children.

> Why not sometimes include poems in your regular reading to the class session?

• It gives access to a highly intense use of language and thus can improve children's language development.

• Because poetry works through hint and allusion it can develop children's abilities to go beyond the literal in their understanding of text.

• It gives access to the most intense expression of human joy, grief, love, etc.

• Its use of language can teach invaluable lessons about reading. Rhyme, for example, we now know to be crucial to children's reading development.

The power of poetry has been well summed up by Charles Causley:

> *All poetry is magic. It is a spell against insensitivity, failure of imagination, ignorance and barbarism. The way that a good poem 'works' on a reader is as mysterious, as hard to explain, as the possible working of a charm or spell. A poem is much more than a mere arrangement of words on paper, or on the tongue. Its hints, suggestions, the echoes it sets off in the mind, and its omissions (what a poet decides to leave out is often just as important as what he puts in) all join up with the reader's thoughts and feelings and make a kind of magical union.*

Even if you accept the potential benefits of introducing your children to poetry, you may not feel particularly confident about two aspects: which poetry to use and what to do with it.

*Selecting poetry*

Perhaps the two best sources of information about poetry which will appeal to children are:

• Kaye Webb, *I Like this Poem* (Puffin, 1977)
• Morag Styles and Pat Triggs, *Poetry 0–16* (Books for Keeps, 1988)

Kaye Webb's collection is a unique anthology of poetry chosen by children for children. Thus it provides an extensive collection of poems that children are likely to enjoy. Each poem is also accompanied by a comment from the child who has chosen it, explaining why. These comments give us a very clear picture of what it is about certain poems that appeals to child readers. The comments go far beyond the simplistic 'Because it's funny' and suggest that, given the opportunity, children can be very skilled critics of poetry.

*Poetry 0–16* suggests and reviews a wide range of poetry collections and anthologies from oral and traditional poems to poems featuring word play. It is interspersed with information boxes about individual poets and also includes a number of interesting and useful articles about teaching poetry.

*Using poetry*

There are a number of books available which explore possible ways of helping children respond to poetry. Particularly recommended are:

• Jan Balaam and Brian Merrick, *Exploring Poetry 5–8* (NATE, 1987)
• Sandy Brownjohn, *Does It Have to Rhyme?* (Hodder & Stoughton, 1980). (Brownjohn has also two other useful books in this series.)
• Pie Corbett and Brian Moses, *Catapults and Kingfishers: Teaching Poetry in Primary Schools* (Oxford University Press, 1986)

---

Help in choosing poetry

---

Get your children to compare their reasons for liking particular poems with the reasons given in this book. Some interesting and useful debate can arise from this.

One dimension of poetry in primary classrooms will also be children's writing of poetry. Sandy Brownjohn's books and also her *Word Games* series give plenty of ideas about how to do this. Five simple ideas are given below:

1. Group poems

Each member of the group writes one sentence beginning with the same phrase, e.g. 'Happiness is ...'. These put together make a poem.

This can be varied by every second line beginning with 'It is ...', or each line could be slightly different, e.g. 'I like Monday / Tuesday / etc. because ...'

2. The furniture game

This is a descriptive exercise. Take a thing or a person. On each line say:
  what piece of furniture it reminds you of,
  what time of day,
  what kind of fruit,
  what sort of weather,
  what kind of animal, etc.

For example:
  *My grandma's like an armchair, warm and cosy near the fire,*
  *Like storytime before the night when everyone is tired.*
  *She's like a winter apple, wrinkled but yet sweet,*
  *A rich white blanket-snowy day, a cat on velvet feet.*

> This was written by Christopher, a nine-year-old I once taught.

This can be played as a game by the writer choosing someone in the class to write about but not actually mentioning the name in the poem. The rest have to try to guess who it is. The writer wins if they can guess; in other words the images have to be strong and richly suggestive.

3. Sensing emotions

Think of an emotion, such as fear, happiness, anger, and write a poem about this emotion according to this formula:
  What colour is this emotion?
  What does it taste like?
  What does it smell like?
  What does it look like?
  What does it sound like?
  What does it feel like?

For example:
  *My fear is red as the evening sky,*
  *It tastes of black, burned toast.*
  *It smells of bonfires, looks like bonfires,*
  *Sounds like an animal about to die.*
  *It's jagged, harsh and makes me cry.*

> Written by ten-year-old Sophie. As with all poetry ideas, you need to try them for yourself before using them with children.

4. Prepositions

Think of seven different prepositions, e.g. over, under, through. Then think of an object. Write a seven-line poem, each line of which has one preposition plus your object. The aim of this is to get different viewpoints on the same object.

> This idea can also introduce children to aspects of grammar, including prepositions and prepositional phrases.

For example:

*In my room I feel at ease.*
*Through my room run dreams.*
*Outside my room the world goes by.*
*Inside my room I stay and sigh.*
*Above my room the seagulls wheel.*
*Below my room the family talk*
*While across my room the moonlight steals,*
*And carries me away.*

### 5. Cinquain

This is a five-line poem which either has a strictly controlled number of syllables (2, 4, 6, 8, and 2), or in which each line serves a precise function. For example:

| | |
|---|---|
| title word: | *Pike* |
| describe it: | *Steely grey* |
| comment upon it: | *Awaits its prey* |
| feeling about it: | *Death dealing impostor* |
| summary: | *River shark* |

### Becoming aware of bias

Most of what we read, especially those texts which deal with supposed 'facts', may actually be propaganda. This is simply because all texts are written by someone and that person is certain to be a member of a particular political, social, religious or racial group and therefore have to some extent that political, social, religious or racial world view. Consequently what he/she writes is not objective. This does not mean that such a writer is deliberately intending to mislead readers (although he/she may be, of course) but he/she may simply not recognize the perspective from which the writing comes.

> A good way of understanding this is to examine daily newspapers and compare their treatment of current news stories.

*Features indicating bias in texts*

Bias in texts is, therefore, virtually universal. Your aim as a teacher should be to enable children to get beneath the surface of a text and become aware of the perspective from which it is written. To do this, you need to be able to be sufficiently critical a reader yourself. You need to know the features to look for in texts which indicate partiality. What are these features?

Examine these two passages, each of which describes the start of the campaign of Bonnie Prince Charlie in 1745:

Passage 1

> *On the 25th July the prince's flag was raised at Glenfinnan. This time no gilt ball fell as the red and white silk banner was unfurled.*

> *It was held by the Marquis of Tullibardine. So old was this chief that two men had to help him raise it.*

> *Here now gathered the Camerons, the clan of the 'Gentle Lochiel', the Stewarts of Appin, the Macdonalds of Glencoe, and many another Highland clan.*
> MEIKLE (1949, p. 204)

Passage 2

> *Prince Charles Edward Stuart raised his standard at Glenfinnan in the western glens. To his chagrin and surprise the whole of the Highlands did not immediately leap to arms. Some of the most powerful families, like the Macdonalds of Sleat who had been out in the 1715, declined to join him ... Their caution was fully justified by events.*
> SMOLT (1969, p. 208)

You might notice the following differences:

*Style and grammatical structure*
Meikle uses three paragraphs to Smolt's one. The effect of this is to give extra significance to the events recounted in each paragraph. Meikle also uses a more 'flowery' style ('the red and white silk banner was unfurled'; 'Here now gathered...'). The effect of this is to make the events described sound more heroic and momentous.

*What is included and what is left out*
Meikle lists the clans which joined the Prince, whereas Smolt only mentions those which did not.

*Vocabulary choice*
Smolt chooses vocabulary to suggest a more negative tone, 'declined', 'caution'.

These three features of vocabulary, grammar and selection of events are those in which bias in texts is most commonly seen.

> Children need plenty of practice in applying these analysis systems. They can come up with some surprising insights.

## Textual structure and conventions

**Text structures**

There has been an increasing interest in the idea of encouraging children to write for a particular purpose, for a known audience and in an appropriate form. However, what constitutes an appropriate form is often dealt with in very general terms such as the listing of different types of texts. In the original version of the National Curriculum for English, for example, the attainment targets for writing included the requirement for children to 'write in a variety of forms for a range of purposes and audiences' (D.E.S., 1990, p. 13) This is exemplified by the suggestion that they might 'write notes, letters, instructions, stories and poems in order to plan, inform, explain, entertain and express attitudes or emotions'.

Text types

This listing of text types implies that teachers and children know what distinguishes the form of one text type from another. At a certain level, of course, this is true – we all know what a story is like and how it differs from a recipe, etc. Most of us are aware that a narrative usually has a beginning, a series of events, one or more complications and an ending in which these are resolved. Many teachers discuss such ideas with their pupils, spending time working on openings or endings of narratives for instance. It is still relatively rare, however, for teachers of primary pupils to discuss non-fiction texts in such a way – drawing on our knowledge of the usual structure of a particular text type to improve our children's writing of that form.

Recently a group of linguists including Gunther Kress, Jim Martin, Joan Rothery and Frances Christie have argued that our implicit knowledge of text types and their forms is quite extensive and one aspect of their work has been to make this implicit knowledge more explicit. These theorists are often loosely referred to as 'genre theorists' and their work is known as genre theory.

An approach to genre theory

> A good introduction to genre theory can be found in Littlefair, A. (1988), *Reading All Kinds of Writing*, Open University Press.

## A functional approach to language

The genre theorists base their work on a functional approach to language. Such an approach looks at the ways in which language enables us to do things. It argues that we develop language to satisfy our needs in society. Based on Michael Halliday's work (e.g. Halliday 1985) on children's language, a functional language approach argues that as we use language several things happen. We learn language, learn through language and learn about language.

We learn language by using language. If we think about our language development from our earliest years we can see that we learn how to use language largely through using it. We refine and add to our vocabulary, for example, by constant exposure to other language users with whom we interact. As we get older we add to our knowledge of our language through reading and writing as well as through talking.

We also use language to interact with our world and increase our knowledge of it. We develop concepts, we ask questions, we make things happen through the medium of language. We learn through language.

As we use language we acquire unconscious, implicit knowledge about how language itself works. Young children, for example, usually learn about plurals and begin to add an -s to the ends of words in their speech long before they are formally taught plurals in grammar lessons. Similarly most children learn to distinguish between past and present tense in their language usage and use tenses appropriately before any formal instruction in this area. As we use language we learn about language. We now recognize that children come to school with an implicit knowledge of language structures and their usage.

> This moving from implicit to explicit knowledge is the underlying idea behind what has become known as KAL work (Knowledge about language).

A functional language approach argues that our implicit knowledge about language should be brought out into the open so that we can use it in our classrooms. One area of implicit knowledge that can be used in this way is our knowledge about genre.

## What is genre?

Over the last few years more teachers have become aware of the term *genre* as the work of certain teachers and academics has become more widely known. Just a few years ago any of us asked to define genre would have probably replied in terms of book or film genres. We are all familiar with the idea that certain books or films have common characteristics which allow us to categorize them as 'romance' or 'murder mysteries' or 'westerns' or 'horror' and so on. The genre theorists would argue that these are just a few of the many different genres that operate in our societies and that the term genre can be applied to a much wider range of language-based activities.

They see all texts, written and spoken, as being 'produced in a response to, and out of, particular social situations and their specific structures' (Kress & Knapp, 1992, p.5) and as a result put stress on social and cultural factors that form a text as well as on its linguistic features. They see a text as always a social object and the making of a text as a social process. They argue that in any society there are certain types of text – both written and spoken – of a particular form because there are similar social encounters, situations and events which recur constantly within that society. As these events are repeated over and over again certain types of text are created over and over again. These texts become recognized in a society by its members, and once recognized they become conventionalized. If we take, for example, forms of greeting we can see how this operates. If we met an acquaintance in the street a common exchange might go:

> *Oh. hello. How are you?*
> *I'm fine thanks. How are you?*
> *Fine ... I'm fine. We must get together for a drink sometime.*
> *Good idea. I'll ring you*
> *Great. Look forward to it. Nice to see you. Bye.*

We all recognize this conventional type of exchange and implicitly know the responses that are expected of us. We know that we usually respond briefly and counter question when queried about how we are. Yet nobody has ever explicitly taught us this text. We have learnt it through usage when similar purposes (acknowledging someone's presence without really getting involved in a conversation) for creating such a text have occurred. If our purpose was different (if, for example, we wanted to get involved in a more intimate conversation) we would structure our text in a different way. Our lives are full of such examples, when similar purposes and situations produce similar texts.

The genre theorists argue that texts have 'a high degree of internal structure' (Kress, 1982, p.98) which largely remains invisible to the reader because when texts have become conventionalized (with recognizable rules and forms) they appear to have an existence of their own – they appear natural. Genre theory looks at these larger textual structures of a whole text as well as the language features within these larger structures.

Many genre theorists go on to argue that not only can we recognize generic structures but that the implicit knowledge we all have of generic structures should be made explicit and that knowledge of these forms and of their social meanings can and should be taught.

### Purpose and genre

Genre has been defined by many commentators. It is defined by some as being the schematic structure found in a text but more commonly it is argued that the purpose of a text influences the form that text will take. Thus the purpose of the communication is central to a definition. Genre theory claims that texts (written or spoken) are structured according to their purposes and texts with the same purpose will have the same schematic structure.

Of course, this does not mean that there is no creativity involved in producing texts, but simply that the creation takes place within boundaries.

What does this idea of generic structures being determined by purpose actually mean? Let's take a text type we are all familiar with – instructions. The purpose of instructions is to tell someone how to do

Text structure is determined by purpose.

something, as in recipes, instruction leaflets with machines, D.I.Y. leaflets and so on. This purpose gives rise to the particular form of these texts – they have to make clear what it is you are doing or making, what materials you need to achieve this aim and the steps you need to take to reach a successful conclusion. It would not make it easier to achieve the purpose if, for example, the steps were given first, then you were told the list of materials you needed and finally you were told what it was you were making. The schematic structure of instructions helps achieve its purpose and is therefore usually:

- goal
- materials
- steps to achieve the goal (usually in time sequence)

You will be aware of such a structure in recipes and D.I.Y. guides. You may not have been explicitly aware of this structure but if you examine instruction texts you will see that, on the whole, they follow the pattern outlined above. You will also be using a similar generic structure when you give any spoken instructions. If you imagine giving instructions to your class at the beginning of a session you might say something like this:

- *Today we're going to finish writing our stories,* (goal)
- *so you'll need your jotters, pencils, line guides and best paper.* (materials)
- *When you've got those sorted out, get on and see if you can finish your first draft. Then you can share it with your writing partner or with me and discuss any alterations you think need to be made. Don't forget to check spellings at the end. OK, off you go.* (steps)

It is highly unlikely that you consciously planned to use, or were even aware of using, this schematic structure but your purpose (to tell the children what to do) meant that you automatically used the appropriate structures – using such a structure came naturally. When we look at how the schematic structure of a text helps it achieve its purpose we are considering its genre.

### Genre and culture

We said earlier that the creation of a text takes place within a culture or society. It is within a certain society that we have a purpose for creating a text and that purpose will give rise to a text produced in a particular genre. This means that if genres are formed within societies they can vary from society to society even if the purpose is the same. A good example of this is the genre of shopping. The purpose of the language interchanges accompanying shopping within any society is to purchase goods and commodities. Within our Western European society the generic structure of a shopping text would generally follow a form something like:

- mutual greeting      *Good morning.*
- query      *Can I help you?*
- shopping request      *I'd like ...*
- granting of request      *Certainly. What colour would you like?*
- statement of price      *That will be ...*
- completing transaction      *Thank you. Goodbye.*

However, in different societies different norms are expected. There may, for instance, be an expectation that some bartering over the price will occur or that extended pleasantries will be expected before any mention of a transaction is broached. In these circumstances a different text with a different generic structure from the Western European model will be found. The purpose is the same, the genre is the same but the generic structure will be different. It is perhaps when we enter different societies that we become most aware of how 'learnt' the generic structures which we take for granted in our own society really are. We have all had experiences of situations where we have not 'known the script', say when ordering a meal in a foreign country, and we have been aware of making the wrong responses, getting the pace wrong and so on. We become aware that text structures are not automatic or natural but are learnt.

Attempting to use the Western European generic structure in a different culture will often result in the purpose not being achieved.

**Genre and register**

Texts can differ not only according to the cultures in which they occur and according to their purpose (and thus their overall structure, i.e. genre) but also according to the particular situations (or contexts) within which they are created. Within a particular situation a text will be created, with a particular generic structure which has its own unique register. Genre refers to the overall structure and form of a text. The term *register* refers to the particular choices about language which are made as the text is created. These choices will depend upon several contextual features, each of which has been given a term in functional grammar. These features are:

* the tenor, that is, the relationship between the participants, text producers and receivers
* the mode, that is, the channel of communication being used: for example, speech or writing
* the field, that is, the subject matter of the text

*Tenor*

The tenor of a text depends on the relationship between the participants in the text creation, the producer of the text and its recipients or audience. The tenor can range from formal to informal, friendly to unfriendly, etc. and is influenced by such factors as the relative status of the participants, how well they know each other, how they feel towards each other, their relative ages. These factors will be reflected in the language used ranging from the use of intimate forms of address, the use of personal pronouns and the use of colloquial terms through to a much more formal use of language.

*Mode*

The channel of communication is either written or spoken but it is also influenced by the distance in time and space between the participants, whether the communication is face to face or consists of something recorded to be read or listened to at some later date, whether the communication accompanies the action as it happens or is distanced from it. For instance, are you discussing where to hang a picture with your partner as you stand with a hammer and nail in your hand, are you discussing this as you stand in front of the print shop window or are you describing the discussion to a friend after it has taken place and the picture hung?

*Field*

The field refers to the subject matter of the text – the what, who, when,

Texts and language choices

Tenor, mode and field

how, why, where, etc. It will give rise to specific vocabulary relating to the subject matter.

These three factors interact to give a text its particular register. To make all this more concrete, an example will help. Let us imagine you wish to argue the case for replacing the reading scheme currently used in your school. Your purpose will be to persuade someone else to your point of view. You will use a persuasive genre and the generic structure will look something like the following:

- an opening statement (your thesis)
- reasons and/or evidence to back up your point of view (points and elaboration)
- a summary and a restatement of your opening position (reiteration)

This overall generic form would stay the same whether you were talking to your headteacher or to a parents' meeting but the register of the text would vary. You would be likely, for example, to use a more technical vocabulary when talking to the headteacher. We can see from this example that whilst the genre of the text determines the overall internal structure of the text (thesis, arguments, reiteration) the register will determine the exact language that will be found in the talk to the headteacher or the talk to parents.

### Written genres in the classroom

Different theorists have categorized the types of written genres we commonly use in the classroom in different ways. Collerson (1988), for example, suggests a separation into *Early genres* (labels, observational comment, recount, and narratives) and *Factual genres* (procedural, reports, explanations, and arguments or exposition), whilst Wing Jan (1991) categorizes writing into *Factual genres* (reports, explanations, procedures, persuasive writing, interviews, surveys, descriptions, biographies, recounts and narrative information) and *Fictional* (traditional fiction and contemporary modern fiction).

There is, however, a large measure of agreement as to what the main non-fiction genres are and the most useful categorization of non-fiction genres is probably that identified by the Sydney linguists (Martin & Rothery, 1986) and subsequently developed during work in Australian schools (Callaghan & Rothery, 1988; Macken et al, 1989). As part of the work of this group, non-fiction texts were collected and analysed, including many examples of children's school scripts. From this they identified six important non-fiction genres which we use in our culture and discovered that in school one of these genres was overwhelmingly predominant.

The six main types of non-fiction genre they identified were:

- recount
- report
- procedure (instructions)
- explanation
- argument
- discussion

The most widely used of these genres in school appeared to be recount – that is, children spend a good deal of their writing time narrating a series of events. This contrasts with adult experience, where narration is

*The main non-fiction genres*

Teachers often set children writing tasks which they hope will produce different types of genres. Yet children do not always respond appropriately. The examples on pp. 24–25 of instructional and explanation writing show this well. Teachers need to know about the features of these texts in order to help children produce them.

See *Check your knowledge* for a detailed analysis of the structural and language feature of these text genres.

not widely used in writing (it is used much more in speech) but other genres, such as argument, figure much more prominently.

Following this line of thought, it would seem to be a good idea for teachers to take steps to ensure that their pupils were more systematically introduced to a wider range of genres in school. Explicitly discussing with children the structures and language features of a range of genres also seems to be a useful line for teachers to follow.

## Grammar and punctuation

The structures and workings of phrases

### Phrases

Phrases are structural elements at a level between the word and the clause, slots in the grammatical system which we can fill with one or more words according to certain rules. Phrases can contain only one word or many words but they are not just any groups of words, of course. Grammar organizes their boundaries and their internal behaviour. Try picking out the phrase-boundaries in this sentence.

> *All alone in her room my mother was watching a short programme on television.*

You have several possible choices in splitting this sentence into phrases:

> *All alone in / her room / my mother was / watching a short programme / on television.*
> *All alone / in her room / my mother / was watching / a short programme / on television.*
> *All alone in her / room my mother / was watching a / short programme on / television.*

If you chose the second one of these, then you have correctly sensed the organizing rules by which English grammar creates phrases. Looking at these phrases in greater detail will show why the boundaries come where they do.

The phrases *my mother* and *a short programme* have a similar structure. Each contains a noun (*mother*, *programme*) whose meaning is made more precise by the other word or words in the phrase. The nouns are essential elements; without them, the meaning in each phrase would vanish. Omitting these nouns would not leave us with a satisfactory sentence:

> *All alone in her room my was watching a short on television.*

But if we use only these nouns we can keep the essential meaning of the sentence:

> *All alone in her room mother was watching a programme on television.*

The same is true for the phrases *all alone* and *was watching*. The sentence would make sense if we missed out one of the two words from each phrase. Which of the following two alternatives is best?

> *Alone in her room my mother watching a short programme on television.*
> *All in her room my mother was a short programme on television.*

Some phrases, therefore, are designed so that a single word acts as the essential element within the phrase. The other words in the phrase are

The adjective *alone* can be used by itself without disturbing the meaning too much; the word *all* cannot. In the case of the verb we have to change it to make the sentence grammatical (*watched* would sound better than *watching*). Nevertheless the verb *watch* is still able to work on its own without significantly changing the meaning. The same is not true if we only keep the verb *was*.

subordinate elements to this principal word. Other phrases do not work like this. Take the phrase *in her room*, for example. If we used one word only from this phrase, the meaning would not be preserved:

> *All alone in my mother was watching a short programme on television.*
> *All alone her my mother was watching a short programme on television.*
> *All alone room my mother was watching a short programme on television.*

The two sections of this phrase – *in* and *her room* – are both equally important and cannot work independently.

Phrases therefore can be divided into two groups: those which include an essential key word and those in which the words are equally important. There are four types of the first kind of phrase, each of which gains its identity from the key word's word-class. These are the noun phrase (*my mother* and *a short programme*); the verb phrase (*was watching*); the adjective phrase (*all alone*); and the adverb phrase (there are none in this sentence, but there might have been if mother had been watching the television very enthusiastically.)

There is only one type of the second kind of phrase. It is introduced by a preposition and is known as the prepositional phrase (*in her room*). We will now look at each type of phrase in more detail.

*The adjective phrase*
Adjectives can come either before the noun in a noun phrase:

> *the **wrong** trousers*

or after certain verbs:

> *Gromit was **worried**.*

In the second example, the key word in the phrase *was worried* is an adjective and therefore this phrase is called an adjective phrase. We could make it more complex by adding an adverb in front of the key word.

> *Gromit was **very** worried.*

*The adverb phrase*
An adverb phrase may contain only one kind of word – an adverb.

> *Gromit ran **quickly**.*

*The prepositional phrase*
A prepositional phrase begins with a preposition (in the pre-position) followed by a word or words to complete the phrase. It can be constructed in several ways:
- with a preposition followed by a noun phrase: *in the garden; under the table*
- with a preposition followed by an adverb: *over there*
- with a preposition followed by an adjective: *at best*

*The noun phrase*
Noun phrases have a noun as their key word.

> *My grandmother,*
> *Gromit,*
> *the very last day*

As with adjective phrases, we can make the adverb phrase more complex by adding other words (always adverbs) in front of the key word (or, just occasionally, after the key word).

*Gromit ran **very** quickly.*

*Gromit ran **even more** quickly.*

*Gromit ran **very** quickly **indeed**.*

Pronouns can take the place of nouns so it is also possible for noun phrases to have pronouns as their key words.

*She* (instead of *my grandmother*),

*he* (instead of *Gromit*),

*it* (instead of *the very last day*).

In noun phrases where the key word is a noun, there are many ways in which we can put words in front of this. Most obviously, we can use an article:

*the pig, a pig*

or a determiner:

*this pig, our pig, which pig?, some pig*

We can also put words in front of the determiner:

*another of our pigs*

and after it:

*another of our old pigs*

We could also say more about the noun by using adjectives:

*another of our old, smelly pigs*

and this could, in theory, go on for ever. Putting words in front of the key word in a noun phrase allows us to build up, with each word added, a more precise definition of the key word.

We can also add information about the key word after it occurs in the phrase:

*the pig in the corner*
*the pig with the well-scrubbed skin*

Again this could go on, in theory, for ever, with each new part to the noun phrase building up an ever more precise picture of the noun being referred to.

*The verb phrase*
A simple verb phrase consists of just a single verb:

*run, climb, think, hope*

Because it carries the main burden of meaning this verb is referred to as the lexical verb. A lexical verb may be inflected (changed) in certain ways. Firstly, it may carry the morpheme which shows the third person singular present tense. This normally involves adding the letter -*s*.

*he runs, she climbs, he thinks, she hopes*

This inflection is necessary because of a rule which demands that the verb must agree with the noun phrase which performs its action when that noun phrase is third person singular (*he, she, one, it, David, the cat,* etc). In the case of nouns which are not third person singular, the verb must also agree – but it does this by not adding the inflection.

*we run, they climb, you think, we hope*

In verb phrases containing only a lexical verb, the only other inflection possible is the adding of the morpheme indicating past tense – normally the letters -*ed*.

*I climbed, you hoped*

Tense, then, is indicated by inflection – by changing the shape of a verb by adding (or not adding) a morpheme.

Of course, many English verbs are irregular, changing their shape in different ways to express past tense:

*I ran, you thought.*

**Auxiliary verbs**

It is also possible to add other words to the lexical verb. These are called auxiliary verbs and always go before the lexical verb. Together with the tense form, they are responsible for expressing, among other things, the time element of the verb phrase. The three most commonly used auxiliary verbs are *do*, *be* and *have* and they can occur in different forms within the verb phrase:

> *I did run, we are climbing, they have thought, you will hope*

With the introduction of auxiliary verbs, a further inflection to the lexical verb becomes possible: the *-ing* ending. This is used to distinguish between a single action which is complete or is habitual from one which is or was continuous.

> *I ran two miles*                  *I am running along the road*
> *I climb the stairs with a heavy heart*    *I was climbing the hill*
> *I thought for a long time*          *I am thinking about you a lot*
> *Every time this happens I hope*      *I was hoping I had seen the*
>    *it is the last*                       *last of you*

A further change of meaning can be achieved by adding one of another group of auxiliary verbs which express a range of meanings suggesting 'probability', 'possibility', 'obligation', etc.

> *He **might** run in the race.*
> *I **can** climb when I want to.*
> *You **must** think more carefully before you act.*
> *They **may** hope but it still will not work.*

Phrases, then, are constructed on one of two basic principles: those with a key word and those without. Of the first kind, there are noun, verb, adjective and adverb phrases, each built of a compulsory key word and other optional words before, after or on either side of the key word and subordinated to it. Of the second kind, there is the prepositional phrase in which a preposition and another element exist in equal balance within the phrase.

> Though only a part of their meaning, these auxiliary verbs also suggest that an event will occur sometime in the future.

---

### Clauses

A clause is constructed of clause elements, one of which must be a verb phrase. Thus in the clause *My mother watches the television* the verb phrase *watches* connects the other two elements both to itself and to each other.

There may be only one other element in a clause:

> *My mother dances*

or there may be more than one:

> *My mother dances every night*
> *My mother watches the television every night*

but in each case, if we remove the verb phrase, no clause exists. Verb phrases, therefore, are essential to clause construction. Clauses are made up of a verb element (the verb phrase) and one or more other elements, held together in a structured relationship around the verb phrase.

There are seven possible elements of clause structure, including the verb phrase. These are:

- Subject
- Verb
- Direct object
- Indirect object
- Subject complement
- Object complement
- Adverbial

We shall look at each of these in turn.

*Subject*

In terms of its meaning, the subject is normally the element which performs the action expressed in the verb phrase. It usually comes first in the clause:

> ***My mother*** *enjoys her television watching.*

The subject has a direct relationship with the verb element and they must agree. Look at the following:

> *My mother **likes** most programmes. Her friends **like** the same programmes.*

Whether the subject is singular or plural changes the inflection of the verb in the verb element.

Subjects can consist of a one-word noun phrase:

> ***I*** *like my dog.* ***Joanne*** *is a television addict.*

a more complex noun phrase:

> ***The woman with the incredibly blue eyes and the matching handbag*** *winked at me as she left the room.*

or a clause:

> ***The man who was waiting for us*** *had decided to leave before time.*

*Verb*

The verb element expresses the action performed by the subject. 'Action' here does not necessarily mean doing something. It can include feeling, being or becoming.

The verb is the most important element in clause structure. It defines a relationship between itself, the subject and the rest of the clause elements. This relationship will be different depending on the kinds of verb element being used. In the clause: *Gromit is an intelligent dog* the verb expresses the fact that *Gromit* and the *intelligent dog* are one and the same thing. Sometimes, the subject can feel or become the following element:

> *Gromit felt pushed out. He became angry.*

A quite different relationship can be created with the clause if another kind of verb is used:

> *Gromit made a plan.*

The following verb elements show the range:

The dog *bit* the man.

The man *felt* really upset at this.

He *became* ill quite quickly afterwards

Here, the subject does something to the third element. The verb here is called a transitive verb; that is, it expresses something being done directly to the third element, the direct object.

Some clauses do not have a third element at all:

*The plan worked.*

Clauses like these, with only a subject (S) and a verb (V), are the most basic kind of clause in English and are called SV structures. As the verbs in them do not have a direct object they are called intransitive verbs.

The verb element is therefore crucial in forming the clause. There are different kinds of verb element (depending on the verb phrase used) making possible different kinds of clause. The verb element is made of either a simple, one-word, verb phrase:

*Gromit **ran** after the penguin.*

or a more complex one:

*The penguin **might have tried to escape** from Gromit.*

*Direct object*
Some clauses are made of a subject, a transitive verb and a third element:

*Gromit captured the penguin.*

This third element is the direct object (O) and such clauses can be called SVO structures. In these, the subject (the 'actor') typically does something (the 'action') to an object.

The direct object gets its identity as a result of its position in relation to the verb. For example, we could reverse the elements in the clause: *The penguin captured Gromit* and the direct object would now be *Gromit*.

The clauses shown so far have been made in the active voice, that is, they are clauses in which the subject is the actor of the action in the verb. SVO clauses, however, can also be transformed from the active into the passive voice. This is a different structure, equivalent in meaning but with the actor of the verb moved from its role as the subject, and the object of the action moved to the subject position. Compare these clauses:

*Gromit outwitted the penguin.*
*The penguin was outwitted by Gromit.*

The meanings here are identical. In the second clause, the subject of the first (*Gromit*) is at the end of the clause and the direct object (*the penguin*) has moved to subject position. The preposition *by* has also been introduced.

Passive clauses are those in which the 'actor' of the action in the verb, becomes the 'agent' of the action in the equivalent passive structure, while the object of that action becomes the grammatical subject of the passive clause.

> Children sometimes, not surprisingly, find the passive a difficult construction to master.

A direct object could easily be the subject if we were to move it to the other side of the verb. So it too consists of a noun phrase.

*Indirect object*
In the clause: *Wallace gave Gromit a fresh bone* there is a direct object (*a fresh bone*) which is given to a recipient (*Gromit*). The recipient is the indirect object. Like the direct object, an indirect object consists of a noun phrase.

*Subject complement*
The subject complement says what the subject is, or is feeling, becoming, seeming, etc. It follows particular verbs, the most common of which is the verb *be*.

> *Gromit was **pleased**.*
> *The penguin was **not very pleased**.*

These clauses are known as SVC structures, the third element being the subject complement. There are two kinds of subject complement normal in SVC clauses. One is a noun phrase:

> *Gromit is **a very clever dog**.*

The second is an adjective phrase:

> *He was **extremely chuffed**.*

*Object complement*
The object complement is what someone or something is or becomes as a result of an action performed by someone or something else. Look at the following sentence:

> *Wallace made Gromit a happy dog.*

The subject (*Wallace*) performs an action in the verb (*made*) which causes the direct object (*Gromit*) to be, or to become, something else (*a happy dog*); *a happy dog* is the object complement.

Like the subject complement, an object complement can be made of a noun phrase:

> *Gromit called Wallace **Master***

or an adjective phrase:

> *Wallace made him **happy**.*

*Adverbial*
The adverbial tells us where, when, why or how the action in the verb happened.

> *Wallace took Gromit **for a ride**.*
> *Gromit went along **willingly**.*

Adverbial elements consist of adverb phrases of one word or more:

> *Come **here**.*
> *He did it **very quietly indeed**.*

They can also be prepositional phrases:

> *Gromit put the bone **under his bed**.*

By now you will have realized that there is no difference between a clause and certain kinds of sentence. In that case, why do we need to talk about clauses at all? The answer is that some clauses cannot stand on their own as sentences. In discussing sentences, we have to introduce three new terms: simple, compound and complex.

........................................................................................................................

**Elements of sentences**

### Sentences

Sentences are the most complex elements in English grammar. The study of how they work is called syntax. They are produced by combining several elements:

- words and their component morphemes;
- phrases with their words;
- clauses with their phrases.

Sentences contain clauses. Some – simple sentences –contain only a single clause. Others contain more than one clause, and much of the grammar of sentence structure is concerned with the systems which allow clauses to be joined together.

Sentences are possible because the grammatical rules which generate them allow an infinite number of unique structures to be created from a comparatively limited set of structural elements.

**Types of sentences**

*Minor sentences*

Before looking at the range of possibilities these rules offer, we need first to mention a very common sentence type which breaks these rules. These are known as minor sentences and have ready-made shapes which rarely change and which are not easy to describe in the same way as other English sentences.

Some of them are used as responses:

    *Yes.      No.     Sorry!     What?*

Others are used as social utterances.

    *Hello.     Goodbye.     How are you?*

Some are normally found only on notices and signs:

    *LADIES     NO ENTRY     KEEP OFF*

*Major sentences*

Other sentences are known as major sentences, whether they contain one or more clauses. Major sentences are limitless in number because of the productivity of the rules which generate them. Using the elements of clause structure and the rules of grammar, we can produce and understand an infinite number of them.

There are four basic categories of major sentence:

- statements
- exclamations
- commands
- questions

Each has different structural features, as follows:

❑ *Statements*

    *Gromit left the house.*

In this kind of structure the subject (*Gromit*) is followed by a verb (*left*) and then by the rest of the sentence.

> Simple sentences contain only a single clause (like those used earlier in this section). Compound sentences contain two or more clauses, joined in a chain. Complex sentences also contain more than one clause, but they are joined in different kinds of ways.

❑ *Commands*

    *Leave the house.*

Here the subject (*you*) has been missed out and the verb mood changed to imperative.

❑ *Exclamations*

    *What a stupid thing to do!*

Here *what* has been used in place of *it was* in the equivalent statement.

❑ *Questions*

• 'Yes/No' type (because they expect a yes-or-no answer):

    *Did Gromit leave the house?*

Here the auxiliary verb *did* has been swapped to the other side of the subject *Gromit*, making a statement into a question.

• 'WH' type (because a WH-word – what, when, who, why, where, how, etc. signals the need for information):

    *Who left the house?*
    *Where did Gromit go?*
    *Why did Gromit leave the house?*

Here, apart from the introduction of the WH-word and, in two cases, the auxiliary verb *did*, the order of elements in the sentences has been reorganized from the equivalent statement form.

• 'Either/or' type (because an alternative answer is possible):

    *Was it Gromit who left the house or Wallace?*

Here the auxiliary verb *was* has been swapped around its subject *it* and the word *or* has been introduced.

• 'Tag' type (because a statement has been made into a question by adding a tag):

    *It wasn't Gromit who left the house, was it?*
    *It was Gromit who left the house, wasn't it?*
    *Gromit left the house, didn't he?*
    *Gromit didn't leave the house, did he?*

Here the tag is made of an auxiliary verb plus a subject. Notice that positive statements are followed by negative tags, and vice versa.

*Joining clauses*

**Multi-clause sentences**

Simple sentences contain a single clause, but it is possible to construct sentences which contain more than one clause. Look at the following simple sentences:

    *Gromit was very angry.*
    *He thought that Wallace did not want him any more.*

There are several ways in which these sentences can be joined together:
• By joining them with a conjunction: *Gromit was very angry because he thought that Wallace did not want him any more.*

- By swapping the order around: *Gromit thought that Wallace did not want him any more and was very angry.*
- By embedding one sentence within the other: *Gromit, who thought that Wallace did not want him any more, was very angry.*

The ways in which clauses can be joined tells us a lot about the power of the grammatical systems of language. Basically, clauses can be joined in one of two ways: they can be put next to each other or put one inside the other.

### Compound sentences

The simplest way to join clauses is to put them next to each other, using a joining-word to cement them into a larger, single, unit:

*Gromit was upset **but** Wallace did not seem to care.*
*Wallace gave away Gromit's room **and** the penguin moved in.*

Sentences in which two or more clauses are joined to each other like this are called compound sentences. Each clause is of equal weight with the others in the sentence. The technical term for the words used to join together the clauses is a conjunction. *And, but* and *or* are the three most common conjunctions.

### Complex sentences

The second way of joining sentences is called subordination. In this, clauses are put one inside the other to make what are called complex sentences. Look at the following two sentences.

*Gromit was very angry.*
*He decided to leave for good.*

These could be joined in the following ways:

*Because Gromit was very angry, he decided to leave for good.*
*When Gromit decided to leave for good, he was very angry.*

In the first of these *Because Gromit was very angry* tells us more about the verb *decided*. It is adverbial and subordinate to the second part of the sentence. In the second example, *When Gromit decided to leave for good* tells us more about his being angry. This part of the sentence is now the subordinate and an adverbial element.

### The relative clause

An important type of subordinate clause is that which refers to only part of one of the clauses being joined. The two sentences above could also be joined like this:

*Gromit, who was very angry, decided to leave for good.*

Here, the subject noun phrase (*Gromit*) has been expanded by the subordinate clause *who was very angry*. This is a very common form of subordination and has its own label: the relative clause. Here are some other examples:

*The penguin **who moved in** turned out to be a crook.*
*He was interested in Wallace, **whose mechanical trousers he wanted to use**.*

Relative clauses can sometimes cause some ambiguity and lead to problems with punctuation. Look at these two sentences:

*The man who was wearing a hat yelled, "Stop thief!"*
*The man, who was wearing a hat, yelled, "Stop thief!"*

Both of these have exactly the same structure, with a relative clause *who was wearing a hat* expanding the subject of the sentence *the man*. However, they suggest different meanings. In the first, the relative clause distinguishes this man from other men.

*The man who was wearing a hat yelled, "Stop thief!" The other men did nothing at all.*

In the second sentence, however, the fact that the man was wearing a hat is added simply to give us a piece of extra information. It is put between commas to show that it is not crucially connected to the noun phrase the man, as it is in the first sentence.

Where the relative clause restricts the meaning of a particular noun phrase, as in the first example, it is called a restrictive relative clause; where it does not restrict the meaning, but simply adds extra information, it is called a non-restrictive relative clause.

........................................................................................................................................

**Punctuation**

The purpose of punctuation

One of the most common misconceptions about the role of punctuation in written English is the idea that punctuation basically tells you 'when to take a breath' when you are reading. In fact, punctuation serves a very important grammatical role. It can also indicate the intonation patterns which a piece of written language would have were it spoken aloud.

Punctuation marks

There are several important punctuation marks, each of which serves a number of grammatical functions. The main marks are:
- capital letters
- full stop
- comma
- semi-colon
- colon
- question mark
- exclamation mark
- brackets
- quotation marks
- apostrophe

The basic rules for the use of each of these are as follows:

*Capital letters*
Use capitals for all proper nouns and all proper adjectives (adjectives derived from proper nouns). The list below provides a quick overview of when capitals should be used.

| | |
|---|---|
| Days of the week: | Sunday, Monday, Tuesday |
| Months: | June, July, August |
| Holidays, holy days: | Christmas, Easter, Diwali |
| Periods, events in history: | Middle Ages, the Renaissance |
| Special events: | the Battle of Hastings |
| Political parties: | Labour Party, Liberal Democrats |
| Official documents: | Magna Carta, Bill of Rights |
| Trade names: | Ford, Kleenex |

| | |
|---|---|
| Formal epithets: | Alexander the Great |
| Official titles: | the Prime Minister, the Lord Mayor |
| Geographical names: | Bay of Biscay, Cape Horn |
| Planets, heavenly bodies: | Earth, Jupiter, the Milky Way |
| Continents: | Australia, South America |
| Countries: | Ireland, Grenada, Sri Lanka |
| Counties: | Devon, Worcestershire |
| Cities, towns, villages: | Exeter, Crediton, Dunchideock |
| Streets, roads, motorways: | High Street, West Road, the M42 |

Use capitals for words like father, mother, uncle, lord when they are parts of titles that include a personal name or when they are substituted for proper nouns (especially in direct address).

*Hello, Uncle David!* (Uncle is part of the name.)
*My uncle David has a new car.*
*Did you know that Lord Somerset owns this land?*
*The lord of this land is a nice man.*
*Where is your mother?*
*Where is Mother Teresa?*

Words that indicate particular sections of the country are proper nouns and should have capitals; words that simply indicate direction are not proper nouns.

*Skiing is popular in the North.*
*Sparrows fly south in the winter.*

The first word in every sentence and the first word in a full-sentence direct quotation should have a capital.

*He never saw a dog he didn't like.*
*The lady shouted up the stairs, 'Come down this minute!'*

Use a capital for the first word in each sentence that is enclosed in brackets if that sentence comes before or after another complete sentence.

*The Labour Party won the 1997 election by a large majority. (They won over 400 seats.)*

Do not use a capital for a sentence that is enclosed in brackets and is located in the middle of another sentence.

*The Labour Party won the 1997 election (for the first time in 18 years) by a large majority.*

Use capitals for races, nationalities, languages and religions.

| | | | |
|---|---|---|---|
| *Muslim* | *Norwegian* | *Canadian* | *English* |
| *French* | *Hebrew* | *Catholic* | *Jewish* |

Use capitals for the first word of a title, the last word, and every word in between except articles (a, an, the), short prepositions and short conjunctions. This rule applies to the titles of books, newspapers, magazines, poems, plays, songs, articles, films, works of art, pictures and stories.

| | |
|---|---|
| *Manchester Guardian* | *Sports Illustrated* |
| *A Wizard of Earthsea* | *The Good, the Bad, and the Ugly* |
| *The Rape of the Lock* | *A Midsummer Night's Dream* |

Use capitals for abbreviations of titles and organizations.

*U.S.A.      NAAFI      M.D.      Ph.D.      NATO*

Do not use capitals for any of the following:
- a prefix attached to a proper noun – *un-British*
- seasons of the year – *winter, summer*
- words used to indicate direction or position – *go north*
- the words god or goddess when they are referring to mythology – *the god of war*

*Full stop*

A full stop is used to end a sentence that makes a statement or gives a command that is not used as an exclamation.

*That man is coming over here.*
*Don't forget to smile when you talk.*

It is not necessary to place a full stop after a statement that has brackets around it and is part of another sentence.

*Lucy gave Jim an earwich (an earwich is one piece of buttered bread slapped on each ear) and ran for her life.*

An ellipsis (three full stops) is used to show that one or more words have been omitted in a quotation.

*"Our father, which art ... for ever and ever, Amen."*

An ellipsis also may be used to indicate a pause in direct speech.

*"Well, Dad, I ... ah ... ran out of petrol ... had two flat tyres ... and ah ... there was a terrible traffic jam in town."*

A full stop should be placed after an initial.

*D. H. Lawrence          J. A. Medwell*

A full stop is also used after each part of an abbreviation.

*Mr.    Mrs.    Ms.    a.m.    p.m.    Dr.    A.D.    B.C.*

This does not apply if the abbreviation is an acronym.

*WRAF (Women's Royal Air Force)*
*radar (radio detecting and ranging)*
*NATO (North Atlantic Treaty Organization)*

*Comma*

A comma is used to separate individual words, phrases or clauses in a series (as long as the series contains at least three items.) There is no comma before the final item if this is preceded by *and*.

*I used a knife, fork and spoon.*
*My luggage included several shirts, two pairs of trousers, a hat and four sets of underclothes.*
*I came in the door, switched on the light, saw a flash and was immediately plunged into darkness.*

Commas are used to enclose an explanatory word or phrase inserted in a sentence.

*Flossing, or cleaning in between your teeth, can be very protective.*

An appositive, a specific kind of explanatory word or phrase, identifies or renames a preceding noun or pronoun.

*My father, **an expert angler**, uses worms to catch trout.*

Commas are used to separate co-ordinate adjectives, that is adjectives that equally modify the same noun.

*I much prefer the small, sweet, round cakes.*

Commas are used to separate contrasted elements from the rest of the sentence.

*We need strong minds, not strong emotions, to solve our problems.*

A comma should separate an adverb clause or a long modifying phrase from the independent clause that follows it.

*If we cannot win the game, at least we'll make it hard for the opposition to win.*

Commas are used to enclose non-restrictive phrases and clauses. Non-restrictive phrases or clauses are those that are not essential or necessary to the basic meaning of the sentence. Restrictive phrases or clauses – those that are needed because they restrict or limit the meaning of the sentence – are not set off with commas. Compare the following examples:

*Rose, who is making funny faces, is my sister.*

(Note: The clause *who is making funny faces* is merely additional information; it is non-restrictive, that is, not required. If the clause were left out of the sentence, the meaning would still remain clear since the name of the girl is given.)

*The girl who is making funny faces is my sister.*

(Note: This time the clause is restrictive. It is needed to identify the girl.)

Commas are used to set off items in an address and items in a date.

*They live at 23 Pine Street, Woolacombe, Somerset.*
*The final deadline was Wednesday, July 4th, 1994.*

Commas are used to set off the exact words of the speaker from the rest of the sentence.

*"I wonder," she mused, "whether there really are wolves in this forest."*

A comma is used to separate an interjection or weak exclamation from the rest of the sentence.

*Hey, will you do me a favour?*
*Yes, I'd be happy to.*

Commas are used to set off a word, phrase, or clause that interrupts the movement of a sentence.

*As a general rule, the safest way to cross the road is via a zebra crossing.*
*That is, however, not always possible.*

Commas are used to separate a series of numbers in order to distinguish hundreds, thousands, millions, etc.

*They wasted £720,806 on a very foolish series of investments.*
*All together £1,789,987 was spent trying to put this right.*

Commas are used to separate a vocative from the rest of the sentence.
(A vocative is the noun that names the person or persons being spoken
to.)

*Don't you realize, George, that you're the very first student to ask for such*
*a thing?*

*Semi-colon*

A semi-colon is used to join two or more independent clauses that are
not connected with a co-ordinating conjunction. (This means that each
of the clauses could stand alone as a separate sentence.)

*I once had a Citroen Dyane; that was the first car I ever owned.*

A semi-colon is used to join two independent clauses within a
compound sentence, when the clauses are connected only by a
conjunctive adverb.

*My friend proudly told me that he had never been beaten at chess; however,*
*he also admitted to having played only children younger than himself.*

*Colon*

A colon may be used to emphasize a word, phrase, clause, or sentence
that explains or adds impact to the main clause.

*Television entertains British children with the most popular theme of the*
*day: violence.*

A colon is used to introduce a list.

*Debbie dropped the bag and out spilled the contents: nail scissors,*
*calculator, car keys, wallet and a ragged old piece of cloth.*

*Question mark*

A question mark is used at the end of a direct question.

*Are your relatives pleased when you visit them?*

No question mark is used after an indirect question.

*My aunt always asks how I am doing in school.*

When two clauses within a sentence both ask questions, one question
mark is used.

*Does your aunt greet you as mine greets me – with a big, wet kiss and a*
*"How old are you now, little lady?"*

*Exclamation mark*

The exclamation mark is used to express strong feeling. It may be
placed after a word, a phrase or a sentence.

*Wow, what a way to go!*
*Please! Tell me that's not true!*

*Quotation marks*

Quotation marks are placed before and after direct quotations or
speech. Only the exact words quoted or spoken are placed within
quotation marks.

*"I really don't know," he said, "whether this year's drought will result in higher food prices, food shortages, or both."*

(Note: The words *he said* are not in quotation marks because the speaker did not say them. Also, the word *whether* is not capitalized because it does not begin a new sentence.)

Quotation marks may also be used:
- to distinguish a word that is being discussed
- to indicate that a word is slang
- to point out that a word is being used in a special way

*I don't think "ain't" is an appropriate word to use here.*
*In order to be popular, she works very hard at being "cute".*

Quotation marks are used to punctuate titles of songs, poems, short stories, lectures, courses, episodes of radio or television programmes, chapters of books, unpublished works, and articles found in magazines, newspapers or encyclopaedias.

Single quotation marks are used to punctuate a quotation within a quotation. Double and single quotation marks are alternated in order to distinguish a quotation within a quotation within a quotation.

*"I have never read 'The Raven'!"*
*"Did you hear him say, 'I have never read "The Raven" '?"*

An exclamation mark or a question mark is placed inside quotation marks when it punctuates the quotation; it is placed outside when it punctuates the main sentence.

*I almost choked when he asked, "That won't be a problem for you, will it?"*
*Did the teacher really say, "Finish this by tomorrow"?*

*Apostrophe*
An apostrophe is used to show that one or more letters have been left out of a word to form a contraction:
- *don't* – *o* is left out
- *she'd* – *woul* is left out
- *it's* – *i* is left out

An apostrophe and *s* can be used to form the plural of a letter, a number, a sign, or a word discussed as a word.

*Dot the i's and cross the t's.*
*You are using too many and's in your writing.*
*The 1990's are a strange decade.*

The possessive form of singular nouns is usually made by adding an apostrophe and *s*.

*The baby's milk*
*Mr. Spock's ears*

(Note: When a singular noun ends with an s or z sound, the possessive may be formed by adding just an apostrophe, e.g. *James' bags*.)

The possessive form of plural nouns ending in *s* is usually made by adding just an apostrophe. For plural nouns not ending in *s*, an apostrophe and *s* must be added.

> *Teachers' classrooms* (more than one teacher)
> *Children's books*

The possessive of a compound noun is formed by placing the possessive ending after the last word.

> *his mother-in-law's* (singular) *husband*
> *their mothers-in-law's* (plural) *husbands*

## How words work

**The making of English**

English is a complex language; it has been shaped by its history and use and will continue to change in response to the uses to which it is put. The words of the English language show a range of historical influences. Some words mark the passing of the various invaders and settlers who have inhabited Britain and others have been borrowed from the lands and colonies which Britons have visited in the last few centuries. English continues to change, adopting new words to cope with modern demands on the language and dropping words no longer required.

The ways in which words are made up and the ways they are spoken and written are the subject of this section. Throughout this section you need to remember that the very vigour and rate of change of the English language has generated many patterns and rules of word formation and pronunciation, and many exceptions. The sounds, symbols and units of meaning which make up words reflect this.

> The presence in our language of new words such as *modem* and *internet* (and *Ofsted!*) testifies to the ever-changing nature of English.

### Phonology – the sound system of spoken words

Phonology is the study of the sound system of a language, in this case the sound system of standard British English spoken in the accent known as received pronunciation (RP). This is the accent usually associated with royalty, government, the law, the church and the BBC. It does not convey any geographical information about the speaker as regional accents do and it is the accent usually taught to foreigners. In fact, very few people speak RP, most using a 'modified' RP.

To study the sounds of a language it is useful to break these up. There are a number of ways of doing this for English.

**Words**

Words can be considered as units of speech which symbolize meaning. Although we all recognize the words of our language when we hear them spoken, breaking up spoken language into words is surprisingly difficult. There are no temporal spaces between most words when we speak. For example: the words *a notion* and *an ocean* are usually pronounced in the same way and only the context establishes what has been said. Spoken words are indicated to the listener by the pattern of stresses and intonations in spoken language and the meanings of words.

> It is hardly surprising that a non-native English speaker cannot always pick out the words of spoken English and can hear utterances like *It's no good at all* as *Snow good a tall*.

**Syllables**

One useful way of breaking up words is into syllables. A syllable is the smallest unit of speech which usually occurs in isolation, consisting of a vowel (like the pronunciation of *I*) or a vowel and consonants (as in the pronunciation of *no, the* and *cat*). Another way to identify syllables is as part of the rhythm of the word. Each syllable is a 'beat' of the rhythm and clapping the beats may help you to identify the syllables. In most words it is fairly easy to identify the syllables but words like *vowel* and *million* cause discussion. In writing it is important to know where to break a word into syllables for the purpose of hyphenation. For instance, it is possible to break *bookmark* between any of the letters, but only *book-mark* would be acceptable when hyphenating at the end of a line.

> Is it vo / wel or vow / el?
>
> Is it mill / i / on or mi / lli / on?

Syllables are one of the earliest ways young children learn to break down words. In doing this children develop the awareness of the patterns of spoken language which will allow them to learn literacy.

**Onset and rime**

Within syllables young children may be able to identify onset sounds (the initial sounds of the syllable) and rimes (the rest of the syllable, not including the onset). This ability to break up syllables is an indication of growing awareness of the sound system of English.

**Phonemes**

The basic units of sound that make up syllables are called phonemes. For example, the single syllable *cat* is made up of the phonemes /c/, /a/ and /t/. A phoneme is the smallest unit of sound that can cause a change of meaning in spoken English. In spoken standard English in an RP accent there are 44 phonemes. The 20 vowel phonemes (sounds) and 24 consonant phonemes (sounds) are listed below.

> These are different in other accents. In northern accents, for example, the middle vowel sound in *cup*, *rough* and *duck* does not appear in RP.

| Vowel phonemes | | Consonant phonemes | |
|---|---|---|---|
| a | is the sound of **a** in **cat** | b | is the sound of **b** in **boy** |
| ah | is the sound of **a** in **father** | ch | is the sound of **ch** in **chip** |
| air | is the sound of **air** in **fair** | d | is the sound of **d** in **dog** |
| aw | is the sound of **aw** in **saw** | dh | is the sound of **th** in **this** |
| ay | is the sound of **ay** in **pay** | f | is the sound of **f** in **fat** |
| e | is the sound of **e** in **jet** | h | is the sound of **h** in **hit** |
| ee | is the sound of **ee** in **see** | j | is the sound of **j** in **jig** |
| eer | is the sound of **ere** in **here** | k | is the sound of **k** in **kin** |
| er | is the sound of **ir** in **bird** | l | is the sound of **l** in **let** |
| i | is the sound of **i** in **ship** | g | is the sound of **g** in **go** |
| ie | is the sound of **ie** in **lie** | m | is the sound of **m** in **me** |
| o | is the sound of **o** in **got** | n | is the sound of **n** in **no** |
| oh | is the sound of **o** in **phone** | ng | is the sound of **ng** in **sing** |
| oo | is the sound of **oo** in **fool** | p | is the sound of **p** in **pig** |
| ou | is the sound of **oo** in **book** | r | is the sound of **r** in **ray** |
| ow | is the sound of **ow** in **how** | s | is the sound of **s** in **so** |
| oy | is the sound of **oy** in **boy** | sh | is the sound of **sh** in **ship** |
| u | is the sound of **u** in **cup** | t | is the sound of **t** in **ten** |
| uer | is the sound of **ure** in **sure** | th | is the sound of **th** in **thin** |
| uh | is the sound of **a** in **sofa** | v | is the sound of **v** in **van** |
| | | w | is the sound of **w** in **wet** |
| | | y | is the sound of **y** in **you** |
| | | z | is the sound of **z** in **zoo** |
| | | zh | is the sound of **zh** in **fusion** |

These phonemes can be precisely represented using the International Phonetic Alphabet, which has a symbol for each sound. This is often used in dictionaries to indicate pronunciations because the normal orthography (the way the sounds are written down) of English has become complicated. Some phonemes can be represented in writing by several different letter combinations. For example: *be, see, sheaf, kiwi, quay, key, people, phoenix*. This complication arouses two types of response. One is to wish that English was written exactly as it sounds. The Simplified Spelling Society campaigns for this. A more common response is to learn as many of the rules and exceptions of English spelling as possible and use reference texts like dictionaries and spellcheckers when writing. The regularities of English spelling usually represent either sound-symbol patterns (phonology), visual patterns (graphology) or patterns of meaning (morphology).

The sound-symbol patterns of English which help a reader identify a written word are the basis of phonics, an approach to teaching reading which emphasizes the sound-symbol regularities of English.

**Stress in words**

The pronunciation of spoken English involves using the 44 phonemes in a number of ways. As well as knowing the way the sounds represented are pronounced, a speaker needs to know where to place the stress in a word. This involves saying a syllable particularly loudly or with emphasis. Correct placing of stress gives spoken English its rhythm and is the basis of rhythm in poetry. The stress is usually indicated by a stress mark (') immediately before the stressed syllable. This is usually included in dictionary entries.

A stressed syllable may be recognized by the sound of the vowel within it. Stressed vowels retain the full vowel quality but those vowels which are not stressed may be pronounced as schwa, for example: *rota, supper* and *eleven*. It is not surprising that young children often find these vowels very difficult to hear and identify when 'sounding out' words.

## Graphology – the alphabetic spelling system

Graphology is the study of the writing system – the spelling rules, the letters and the punctuation of the language. Although the writing system was developed to record spoken English, since the time when spoken English was first written down it has undergone much more rapid change than written English and the written language does not now faithfully represent the sounds of English.

**Graphemes**

The basic unit of written English is the grapheme, for example <a>, <b>, etc. There are 26 graphemes in English, and each may be written in a number of ways – as lower and upper case letters or in different typefaces a, A, a, A. These different representations of the graphemes are called graphs. Graphemes are usually written in angle brackets like this <a> to indicate that they represent the symbol, not the sound.

The spelling rules of English include rules about how words are written in relation to their sounds. For example, which letters are usually silent, and which graphemes represent the phonemes. There are also rules about how the written forms of words change to reflect changes of meaning. The use of derivational and inflectional suffixes (below) involves rules about adding prefixes and suffixes.

Although English spelling is very complicated there is a very high degree of visual regularity. Certain combinations of letters occur again and again and these are known as spelling strings. Knowing these combinations can help the writer to spell correctly. However, these visual regularities may not represent a regular sound, so they are not phonic rules.

**Morphology – word meanings, structure and derivations**

In language, morphology is the study of the structure of words. It includes how words are built up and the job of different parts of words. Words and sentences can be analysed at a morphological level.

Consider this sentence

*The two girls watched the stars appear in the darkening sky.*

Three of these words can be divided into smaller units. *Darkening* can be divided into three parts called morphemes.

*dark-en-ing*

The first part of the word, *dark* could be used in many other words, such as *darkness, darker* and *darkest*. It is a type of morpheme known as a free morpheme because it can stand alone. Some words can be made by combining free morphemes:

*care-less*
*cup-board*
*motor-way*

The other parts of the word *darkening* could not stand alone. The morphemes *-en* and *-ing* are called bound morphemes because they can only be found attached to free morphemes. Bound morphemes can change the grammatical status of a word. At the beginnings of nouns *en-* is used to make them into verbs as in *encircle, entrust* and *enforce*, and at the ends of adjectives *-en* can make them into verbs, as in *lighten, hasten* and *darken*. The morpheme *-ing* can be used to make verbs express continuous action or to make verbs into adjectives: *falling, planning, whispering*. Bound morphemes can also change the meaning of the word. The addition of *dis-* to the word *appear* makes a word of the opposite meaning.

Another common way to consider morphological analysis of language is by using the idea of stems and affixes. The word *untimely* has three morphemes: *un-time-ly*. In this case *time* is not a word, it is the morpheme known as the root or stem of the word *untimely*. The word *time* on its own consists of the single free morpheme *time*. Sometimes the spelling of the stem alters to allow the other morphemes to be joined on, as in *hiding* where the word *hide* is spelt as *hid-* to allow the morpheme *-ing* to be added.

The bound morphemes *un-* and *-ly* are affixes. Affixes which go on the end of the word are called suffixes:

*beauti-ful*
*invest-ment*
*stay-ed*

---

**Working with morphemes**

---

The other two are not so obvious. *Girls* contains two morphemes, the stem *girl* and the plural ending *-s*. *Watched* also contains two, the stem *watch* and the past tense suffix *-ed*.

Affixes which go at the front of the word are called prefixes:

> *trans-continental*
> *im-proper*
> *un-helpful*

We have already seen that prefixes and suffixes (bound morphemes) like *en-* and *-ing* can change the grammatical status of a word to which they are affixed. This is called derivation and can involve the use of derivational suffixes like *-ly*, *-ize* and *-al* to change the word class of a word.

Inflection is the process of changing the form a word to mark a change in meaning. Inflectional suffixes are those which change the grammatical status of the word. It is clear that *boy* and *boys* are not the same word but they are closely related in meaning. The important difference is a contrast signalled by a change in form, which is the addition of the letter *s* in writing and the phoneme /z/. This also expresses a change of meaning.

There are a number of ways of expressing singular/plural contrasts.

> *boy-s* (pronounced s)
> *race-s* (pronounced iz)
> *formula-e* (pronounced ee or eye)
> *men* (vowel changed and pronounced differently)
> *child-ren* (ren added and pronounced)
> *fish* (pronounced like the singular)

All these different forms are different realizations of the same morpheme – the plural morpheme. The same principal applies to other inflections. The morpheme which marks the contrast between past and present tense may also be realized in a number of different ways.

| | |
|---|---|
| *call* | *called* |
| *run* | *ran* |
| *sleep* | *slept* |
| *think* | *thought* |
| *bring* | *brought* |
| *sink* | *sank* |

Morphology is the study of the formation of words, which are made of morphemes. Sometimes they combine to make new words in ways which affect meaning but do not affect other language levels like grammar. However, words also change as a result of inflection and so morphology also affects grammar. In fact, morphemes are the smallest unit of grammar.

*Fish* is an example of a zero morpheme. It contains a plural indicator but this has lost any physical manifestation. *Sheep* and *deer* are other examples.

# Glossary

| Term | Definition | Page |
|---|---|---|
| abbreviation | A shortened or contracted form of a word or phrase | 39 |
| abstract noun | A noun that refers to an abstract concept such as peace or joy | 37 |
| accent | Language variation indicated by pronunciation | 42 |
| acrostic | A poem in which the first letters of each line spell a word | 30 |
| adjective | A word or phrase describing a noun or pronoun | 67 |
| adverb | A word or phrase adding extra meaning to a verb | 72 |
| alliteration | The use of the same consonant at the beginning of words in a line or lines of poetry | 28 |
| anaphora | A reference which refers back to another element in a sentence or text | 36 |
| antonym | A word meaning the opposite of another | 48 |
| apostrophe | A punctuation mark used to indicate omission of one or more letters, or possession | 81 |
| assonance | The use of the same vowel sounds within a line of poetry | 28 |
| blend | The sounds made by two consonants pronounced closely together but each retaining their own distinctive sound | 44 |
| blend words | Words made by combining and abbreviating two words (e.g. *brunch*) | 49 |
| capitalization | The use of capital letters | 76 |
| cataphora | A reference which looks forward to another element in a sentence or text | 36 |
| characters | The participants in a story | 32 |
| chorus | One or more lines of poetry repeated regularly between the verses | 29 |
| clause | A group of words containing a verb, which does not necessarily form a sentence | 69 |
| cohesive tie | A word or group of words which enables links between parts of sentences or texts | 36 |
| colon | A punctuation mark usually used to precede an explanation or a list | 80 |
| comma | A punctuation mark used to separate items in a list or a non-restrictive clause from the main clause | 78 |
| command | A type of sentence conveying an order to act | 74 |
| compound words | Words formed from the joining of two other words (e.g. *breakfast*) | 49 |
| conjunction | A word which connects words, phrases or clauses | 75 |
| connective | A word or phrase which connects clauses in a sentence | 36 |
| couplet | A pair of lines, usually rhyming, which go together in poetry | 29 |
| demonstrative | A pronoun which refers to a particular noun (e.g. *that*) | 42 |
| derivational | Affixes which allow new words to be derived from other words | 86 |
| dialect | A language variety distinguished by distinctive vocabulary and grammar | 42 |
| digraph | Two vowels or consonants which make a single sound when placed together in a word | 44 |
| diphthong | A vowel sound during the pronunciation of which the tongue moves from the position of one vowel sound to that of the other | 45 |
| discussion | A text genre whose purpose is to contrast two or more viewpoints on a particular topic | 34 |
| ellipsis | A form of cohesion in which reference is made by omission | 36 |
| exclamation | A sentence type in which strong emotions are expressed | 74 |

| Term | Definition | Page |
|---|---|---|
| explanation | A text genre whose purpose is to advance a set of reasons for a particular phenomenon | 35 |
| full stop | A punctuation mark used to indicate the end of a sentence | 78 |
| genres | Text types whose form varies according to their purpose | 61 |
| grammar | The rules for the formation and combination of morphemes, phrases, clauses and sentences in a particular language | 73 |
| graph | The physical representation of a grapheme | 84 |
| grapheme | The minimum unit of writing (letter) which may take different shapes (graphs) | 84 |
| graphology | The study of the system of writing shapes in a language | 84 |
| haiku | A particular condensed form of poetry popular in Japan | 30 |
| homograph | Words spelt the same way but pronounced differently and with different meanings | 46 |
| homonym | Words which are spelt and sound the same way but differ in meanings | 48 |
| homophone | Words which sound the same but differ in spelling and meanings | 48 |
| inflection | Changes to words to indicate changes in meaning (e.g. past tense) | 86 |
| instructions | A text genre which gives directions to achieve a goal. | 34 |
| intransitive verbs | Verbs which do not take a direct object | 37 |
| lexical tie | A cohesive tie relying upon the repetition of words or synonyms of words | 36 |
| limerick | A poetic, usually comic, form which has five lines and an AABBA rhyming scheme | 29 |
| long and short vowels | Vowel sounds which are either pronounced long (*bike*) or short (*bit*) | 44 |
| metaphor | A way of describing one thing using terms usually found in descriptions of other things | 28 |
| morpheme | The smallest unit of meaning in a language | 85 |
| morphology | The study of the ways words are formed to represent meanings | 85 |
| narrative | A text form using past tense to retell a sequence of events | 32 |
| onset and rime | Intra-syllabic divisions – e.g. in *bag b-* is the onset and *-ag* is the rime | 43 |
| paragraph | One of a number of blocks into which text is divided to separate units of meaning | 35 |
| personification | A poetic device in which abstract concepts are given human characteristics | 29 |
| persuasion | A text genre with the purpose of convincing the reader of an argument | 35 |
| phoneme | The smallest unit of sound in a language | 83 |
| phonology | The study of the sound system in a language | 82 |
| phrase | A group of words forming a grammatical constituent of a sentence but not containing a finite verb | 66 |
| prefix | An affix which is attached to the beginning of a word to alter its meaning | 86 |
| preposition | A word used before a noun or pronoun to relate it grammatically to another constituent of a sentence | 37 |
| pronoun | A word standing in the place of a noun or noun phrase | 67 |
| proper nouns | Nouns which are the names of people, places or events | 37 |
| punctuation | The system of marks other than letters which indicates elements of intonation and meaning in writing | 76 |
| question | A sentence type which contains an interrogation | 74 |
| quotation marks | Punctuation marks used to enclose direct speech | 80 |

| Term | Definition | Page |
|---|---|---|
| recount | A factual text genre with the purpose of retelling events | 34 |
| reference tie | A cohesive tie in which an element is referred to by a word or group of words | 36 |
| relative pronouns | Pronouns which introduce clauses and relate them to other clauses within the same sentence | 75 |
| report | A text genre whose purpose is to describe and present facts about an object | 34 |
| rhyme | When two words have identical end sounds they are said to rhyme | 28 |
| schwa | The unstressed vowel sound | 84 |
| semi-colon | A punctuation mark used to indicate greater breaks in meaning flow than the comma | 80 |
| sentence | A sequence of words capable of standing alone to make an assertion, ask a question or give a command | 73 |
| simile | A figure of speech which compares one thing with another, using the connector *like* | 29 |
| sonnet | A poetic form of fourteen lines usually used to reflect upon feelings | 30 |
| spatial connective | A connecting word or group of words indicating a spatial relationship (e.g. *next to*) | 36 |
| standard English | A variety of English widely used in writing and having high social status | 42 |
| statement | A sentence type which makes an assertion | 73 |
| stem (root) word | The smallest part of the word to which affixes are attached to make new meanings | 85 |
| stress | The emphasis placed upon part of a word | 84 |
| substitution tie | A cohesive tie in which the word referred to is substituted by another | 36 |
| suffix | An affix which is attached to the end of a word to alter its meaning | 85 |
| syllable | Part of a word, made up of a combination of vowels and consonants | 82 |
| synonym | A word with the same meaning as another | 48 |
| temporal connective | A connective word or group of words indicating a time relationship (e.g. *afterwards*) | 36 |
| tense | A category of a verb which indicates the relationship in time between the utterance and the events reported in the utterance | 48 |
| transitive verb | A verb which takes a direct object | 37 |
| trigraph | A combination of three letters which make only one sound | 44 |
| verb | A word class which indicates an action or the existence of a state | 70 |

# Further reading

## Books and articles mentioned in the text

Balaam, J. & Merrick, B. (1987) *Exploring Poetry 5–8*, Sheffield: National Association for the Teaching of English

Brownjohn, S. (1980) *Does It Have to Rhyme?* Sevenoaks: Hodder & Stoughton

Callaghan, M. & Rothery, J. (1988) *Teaching Factual Writing: A Genre-Based Approach*, Sydney: NSW Department of Education

Collerson, J. (1988) *Writing for Life*, Sydney: PETA

Corbett, P. & Moses, B. (1986) *Catapults and Kingfishers: Teaching Poetry in Primary Schools*, Oxford: Oxford University Press

D.E.S., (1990) *English in the National Curriculum*, London: HMSO

Gowers, E. (1954) *The Complete Plain Words*, London: HMSO

Halliday, M. (1985) *An Introduction to Functional Grammar*, London: Arnold

Kress, G. (1982) *Learning to Write*, London: Routledge

Kress, G. & Knapp, P. (1992) 'Genre in a social theory of language', *English in Education*, 26 (2)

Lewis, M. & Wray, D. (1996) *Developing Children's Non-fiction Writing*, Leamington Spa: Scholastic

Littlefair, A. (1988) *Reading All Kinds of Writing*, Open University Press

Macken, M. *et al.* (1989) *The Theory and Practice of Genre-Based Writing*, Sydney: NSW Department of Education

Martin, J. & Rothery, J. (1986) *Writing Project Report, No. 4*, Sydney: University of Sydney Department of Linguistics

Styles, M. & Triggs, P. (1988) *Poetry 0–16*, London: Books for Keeps

Webb, K. (1977) *I Like this Poem*, Harmondsworth: Puffin

Wing Jan, J. (1991) *Write Ways: Modelling Writing Forms*, Melbourne: Oxford University Press

## Further reading you would find useful

Bain, R., Fitzgerald, B. & Taylor, M. (1992) (eds.) *Looking into Language*, Sevenoaks: Hodder & Stoughton
*A useful collection of articles about language in education arising from the ill-fated Language in the National Curriculum (LINC) project. The writers all have extensive experience of working with teachers to help bring a more explicit attention to language into their teaching and the book is full, not only of insights into language itself, but also into how to teach this in the classroom.*

Crystal, D. (1987) *The Cambridge Encyclopaedia of Language*, Cambridge: Cambridge University Press
*An excellent and comprehensive reference guide to language in all its forms. Although a fairly hefty volume, the entries are written so well it can easily be read for entertainment as well as information.*

Crystal, D. (1991) *Language A–Z* (Books 1 and 2), Harlow: Longman
*Intended for younger secondary school children, these two books are probably the best introductory books about language and linguistics currently available. Written with humour and authority.*

Gannon, P. & Czerniewska, P. (1980) *Using Linguistics: An Educational Focus*, London: Arnold
*The aim of this book is to provide teachers of English with sufficient information about linguistic principles that they are able to intervene sensibly to help children improve their use of the language. Rather heavily written, but a useful introduction to the place of linguistics in education.*

Hudson, R. (1992) *Teaching Grammar*, Oxford: Blackwell
*A very useful account of the grammar of English. Written to include teaching material as well as more theoretical insights. Useful as a guide to making grammar accessible to pupils of all ages.*

McArthur, T. (1992) *The Oxford Companion to the English Language*, Oxford: Oxford University Press
*An enormous volume, which nobody would try to read straight through. Yet the entries are written accessibly and the material covered is absolutely comprehensive.*

Martin, J. (1989) *Factual Writing: Exploring and Challenging Social Reality*, Oxford: Oxford University Press
*One of the key texts of genre theory. Martin here exhaustively analyses the features of factual writing genres and makes a very persuasive case for such knowledge being a necessary part of the teacher's armoury. Difficult reading in places but well worth persisting with.*

Parker, S. (1993) *The Craft of Writing*, London: Paul Chapman
*A useful analysis of types of writing, their structure and linguistic features. Written a little too early to include the important insights into the relationships between social purpose and writing structure which the Australian genre theorists have provided, but still a very useful volume.*

Sealey, A. (1996) *Learning about Language*, Buckingham: Open University Press
*A more recent book on the topic of knowledge about language. Its strength lies in the way it presents a wide range of practical ideas for using many kinds of texts to teach children about language. Such text-embedded teaching is much more likely to be successful than decontextualized approaches to language facts.*

Trudgill, P. (1975) *Accent, Dialect and School*, London: Arnold
*A classic and controversial text. Trudgill is best known for his stalwart defence of the position that there is no 'correct' variety of English but that all dialects are equally correct. If standard English has a higher status, the argument goes, it is for social rather than linguistic reasons. His position is brilliantly argued and illustrated here and, although twenty years old now, there is probably still no better book on the vexed topic of dialect and schooling.*

# Personal learning plan

The **Personal learning plan** is a way of planning and recording your progress through the material covered in this book. Choose an area in the *Auditing your knowledge* section and attempt the questions. Check the extent of your knowledge by referring to the *Checking your knowledge* section. Try to discuss any areas of difficulties with your colleagues and friends. You should reach a point at which you can decide that either you are confident you have a grasp of the relevant knowledge in this area, or you have identified that you need to do some further, more detailed work in this area. Record this in the **Initial Record of Progress** sections below.

If you need to do some more work, check what help is available to you. Perhaps there are sessions planned for these topics in your course programme, or maybe there are optional self-study materials available (the self-study materials in the *Developing your knowledge* section of this book will get you started). Make a note in the **Action Plan** sections below of how you will respond to the needs you have identified. It is important that you are as specific as possible about this. Do not simply assume that 'something will turn up'. You need to plan your own learning in an active way.

Record your progress in the **Update on Progress** sections below. Remember to review these from time to time to make sure you are making progress. It is important to keep up to date with this Personal Learning Plan. Good luck with your learning.

## Using and examining texts

| Initial Record of Progress | Action Plan |
|---|---|
| | |
| | Update on Progress |
| | |

# Textual structure and conventions

**Initial Record of Progress**

**Action Plan**

**Update on Progress**

# Grammar and punctuation

**Initial Record of Progress**

**Action Plan**

**Update on Progress**

# How words work

Initial Record of Progress

Action Plan

Update on Progress

# Looking at children's language

Initial Record of Progress

Action Plan

Update on Progress